SAME SHOES DIFFERENT DOORS

Sukhjit Singh

For book purchase : visit www.sukhforchange.com

ISBN
978-0-9951813-1-1 (Paperback)
978-0-9951813-3-5 (eBook)

Cover design, internal formatting & layout by Hemant Lal
www.AaronProductionsIndia.com

TABLE OF CONTENTS

PREFACE

"The best way to predict the future is to create it."- Peter Drucker

It was a bright and sunny morning in January of 2016. The sun was rising from the horizon, and was trying to peep through the clouds. As I sat on my bed with a cup of tea the scene looked exceptionally beautiful. My favorite shoes were right next to my bed, as is always the case. It was these shoes that took me to different doors, and got me the desired success. In fact, I shared a small story about my journey of immigration with www.settlement.org, and they published the write-up in 2011. The article was titled 'Same Shoes – Different Doors.' That small write-up made me realize how valuable those shoes were to me. Interestingly, the article also won me an iPod Nano.

I would agree that the beautiful scene that day in January looked more stunning because I was within the comforts of my own home. For any immigrant who moves to Canada, buying one's own house is the ultimate dream. You need to incur large expenses upfront and jobs are at a premium. This means that you aren't left with much to afford the luxuries you want to buy for your family. That inspired me to share my story with all of you. If I could inspire just a few immigrants, international students, and refugees to Canada to do the right things and reap success in return, my goal would be accomplished.

When I moved to Canada, I was in the same position as many other immigrants. I was desperately looking for a job, and it had been months now without even a proper interview call. At the same time, I had to also fight against my fear of taking the public transit. I didn't know why, but I was seriously afraid of getting on the bus. Plus, I didn't know what to do once I was on it. To add to the complexity was my social network that kept telling me that a factory job was all I could get for myself. By the way; I have a B.Sc in Computer Engineering and MBA, and the thought of working in a factory made me feel defeated.

In fact, I even got myself a pair of safety shoes. These are my favorite ones, the ones I spoke about earlier. The reason is that it was this very same pair of boots that changed my life. Not only do these shoes remind me of how I decided to refrain from working for a factory, but also how I created a lifestyle for myself that helped me get a spot in the list of RBC's top 25 immigrants award for the year 2013.

This book is an effort to share, with all my readers, a story that will inspire you to meet reality. I have tried to encompass all those things that I think I did right to quickly pass through my days of struggle. My stories will strive to tell you a tale of what you should and shouldn't do as an immigrant.

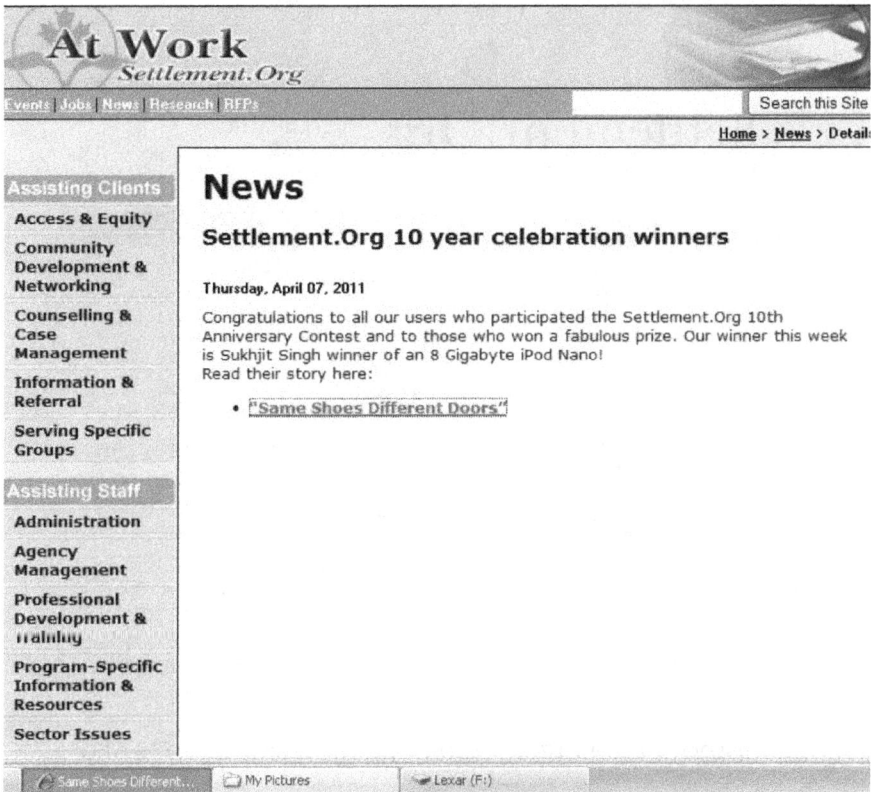

A snapshot of www.settlement.org with news about me winning an iPod Nano.

Same Shoes Different Doors

This is a story of individual (Myself) who wanted to come to Canada for higher studies , but gave up after a refusal in year 1997. Initially thinking that I will never go to Canada. Things changed and this individual (Myself) wanted to really see the country names "Canada ". It was a friend who told the most interesting facts and stories about Canada including the beauty of country, the way of living, multiculturism, opportunities and what not.

A decision is being made that at what stage it will be right to move to Canada and I landed with my wife and daughter Picture looked very blurry as economy was hit hard during that time (July - Sept 2010). Friends told about the real job market and the struggle I may face. But they were right in saying the true picture.

This web site (www.settlement.org) was first explored when I started the process of moving to Canada. It was Google search engine when this web site popped up. Since I start planning to come to Canada, that that was first time in Year 2005

After careful and very meticulously planning (Internet and the web site like www.settlement.org were the most widely used tools for planning) , the day came when we landed in Canada. For entire 5 days, jet lag and the fear of new country kept my indoor. The day I had bet with my wife that I will travel on transit and come back home safely was the last day I stayed in.

I did my research first to see that how strong is this web site, matching the information with other resources available with other web sites.

However I was realizing one very important strength in me, it was my familiarity and knowledge about the various services and programs available for newcomers. Because once the process of immigration was on last stages to immigrate to Canada, I did spent 70% of time to fully explore all the web site links available under all the categories in www.settlement.org , which further helped me to help other by informing about the services from Govt. Of Canada through the web site www.settlement.org.

Now days I use this web site for another purpose, as a Settlement Worker and Information Counselor. I would say that best tool which is multipurpose tool (SWISS KNIFE) for all who wants to start exploring about Canada and for them who are in social service/human service sector as well.

A snapshot of the article about me on www.settlement.org.

ACKNOWLEDGEMENTS

I would like to start by acknowledging the support and encouragement that my friends and family offered to me throughout the process of putting this book together. All of you believed in my story and its ability to help existing as well as aspiring Canadian immigrants. Thank you for always showing me the right path.

My wife (Damanpreet) & daughter (Harjap) need a special mention here as they have been an integral part of my story. Throughout this book, I have made brief mentions about my wife's support in this journey. However, no words could express my gratitude towards her relentless support and understanding. We believe in the concept of 'Soul Mates,' and she only validated that further by being the pillar of the beautiful life we managed to create for our family here in Canada. My daughter, on the other hand, has been an epitome of encouragement and patience. Although being so young, she takes keen interest in my work and encourages me wholeheartedly. Moreover, her patience during our times of struggle allowed us to gradually make our way through those tough days.

My parents have always being so important to me. Thank you papa, mummi for giving me the best possible education and letting me make decisions that were right for me and my family. You have always trusted me, and I hope I have made you proud. I will keep striving hard and continue to do more good work, just to see that pride in your eyes.

I also need to thank Bhavika & Mohit Masand. I met with Bhavika on LinkedIn, and we quickly struck a chord. What surprised me, though, was that Bhavika talked more about her husband than herself. That told me about her love for her husband, but also made me keen to see Mohit. My first meeting with Mohit set the tone for a life-long friendship. I was impressed by his skills, and he agreed to collaborate with me on this book – all of this in the first meeting. Over the last year and a half, he has provided continuous support with editing this book, providing design/publishing tips, and suggesting marketing ideas. The work with this book is over, but our friendship is here to stay.

Tanmay Mathur and Ashesh Jain – can I ever thank you enough? I wanted to click pictures for the cover of this book, and they worked tirelessly to help me find the right picture. We went to almost all buildings and offices that I had visited in the early part of my struggle, busses I had taken to get to successful and not-so-successful meetings, and intersections that shaped my story. Thank you both for being so accommodative and persistent.

Last but not the least; I would like to thank all those great colleagues-turned-friends who have been kind enough to contribute to this book. In no particular order, I would like to express my sincere gratefulness to Dorothy Maciag-Zwolski, Sweety Khanija, Adriane Beaudry, Dilnawaz Qamar, Raghvendra Bagla, and Umbereen Mehmood.

It's been a beautiful journey, and all of these people and many more like them have made it more joyous.

CHAPTER ONE

THE CANADIAN WAY

"And, when you want something, all the universe conspires in helping you to achieve it."

*Y*es; I am a big Bollywood fan - No; I didn't like Om Shanti Om (popular Bollywood movie). For those ardent Bollywood fans, this quote might have reminded them of superstar Shahrukh Khan citing it in the film 'Om Shanti Om.' It actually comes from Paulo Coelho, the celebrated author. From my perspective, though, I could not think of any better way of commencing this book. Coming from India, we are exposed to spirituality at a very early age; and this is one thing that you will always hear from your parents. If you deserve it and if it is meant for you, you shall get it. All you want to ensure is that your desire for the thing is genuine, and you have done enough to be deserving of it. My story from a dreamer in an affluent town of Punjab (North India) to a successful Canadian is reflective of this belief.

Everyone who's a part of the immigrant community knows about the struggles that we have to go through at each stage of our move to this country. However, when these struggling immigrants return to their country for a visit, they present a different picture of their life. That's where my story began too. Punjab is known to be an outward looking state of India, as many young boys and girls decide to set course on an adventure called 'Immigration.' They move to new countries, and do all they could to bring pride to their community (and some dollars in their wallet). Being in Punjab, I used to be introduced to many such individuals who had made it large in the western world, or so were we made to believe. These individuals would be sleekly dressed and would unceasingly speak about their 'White' friends and the frantically large amount of money they have made. That's all that you think of as a young boy, don't you? Money, good clothes, and beautiful friends. It was only recently that I realized that many of those rich Non Resident Indians (NRIs) were actually doing menial jobs in their respective countries to make ends meet. Those good clothes and not-so-true stories were just a façade that they donned to present themselves as successful NRIs (Non-Resident Indians). However fancy and unbelievable their stories, it was my interaction with these NRIs that instigated a desire in me to move to Canada – the land of opportunities.

The 2 a.m. test...

My desire of making it large in Canada was, however, put to the test on a chilly winter morning in New Delhi (capital of India) in the year 1998. For all of you who think India is a warm country, you should visit the north in the months of December and January. That morning at 2 a.m. in New Delhi, I knew what it meant to 'go to the limit' to achieve your dreams. New Delhi was shivering that morning with temperatures plummeting to near freezing point. People around me were covered in layers of warm clothing, and their hands were tightly squeezed into their pockets. Winter scarves shielded most part of their faces, leaving just the eyes uncovered. New Delhi's renowned winter haze was limiting our vision to nothing more than a few meters. So, what exactly was I doing in New Delhi that morning? Let me tell you the story.

With my fascination to move to Canada in search of independence, money, and a new adventure; I had convinced my parents to help me file a student visa application for the country. My father, being one of the most honest public servants in the region, had people who respected him and were willing to help. One of those people was an Immigration Consultant, and he helped me get enrolled in a community college in Northern Ontario and apply for my student visa. However, I received a letter from the Canadian High Commission, New Delhi asking me to appear for an interview. While the letter mentioned the date of the interview, it didn't state the time. So, the norm was that you queue up at the gate of the Canadian High Commission at 2 a.m. in the morning, and hope that you get to see the Visa Officer that day. That's why I had to bear Delhi's freezing cold that morning with all other individuals who were called the same day.

I was excited and nervous at the same time. While I was thrilled about the prospects of getting my visa stamped that day, I was also nervous about being required to speak English for a long duration of time. English happens to be my third language, after Punjabi & Hindi, and I was never really required to speak in English for longer than a couple of sentences.

My excitement for the visa was, however, subdued because of the long wait. My interview happened in the afternoon, and I was made to wait till the evening with a few others. After waiting for a long time, the Visa Offer appeared in front of me to seal my fate. I hadn't convinced him enough about my intention to come back to India after the course, and my Visa was rejected.

Image of the letter by the Canadian High Commission issues in 1998

Canadian Way in The Sultanate of Oman...

How do you feel when something that you have always dreamt of vanishes in a few moments? When you are young and naïve, you think that it is the end of the world. You want to believe that everyone has conspired against you to ensure that you don't achieve your goals. That's how I felt too. I cursed the Visa Officer, and I cursed the country. I had decided to never think of Canada again. There were various other countries that were willing to accept me; why would I want to just think about Canada? With that thought in mind, I started applying for jobs in other countries. At the same time, I also moved on with my life. I started working at a private company in my hometown, and that used to keep me occupied. The large social circle that most of us have in India doesn't generally let us be alone, bored, or depressed. Not only did I have my relatives to connect with after work, I made friends at my job-place too. Hence, I had a large group that I used to share my thoughts and ideas with. If I got any free time during the day, I would use that to randomly apply for openings outside India. I had no inhibitions about any country, and all that I was looking for was the quality of the position. I did not want to get into something that didn't exactly match my profile. This was especially because my life in India was pretty smooth too.

One fine day, I received an interview call from an employment agency that was hiring for an Engineering College affiliated to a Scottish university in Oman. The interview was in New Delhi, and that brought back those bad memories of being in queue outside the visa office at 2 a.m. Thinking of that frigid cold night made a chill run down my spine. However, I knew that I couldn't let the baggage of old memories haunt my future. This was an interesting opportunity, and I didn't want to let it pass. So, I appeared for the interview and it went well. They offered me a position, and before I knew it; I was moving to the Sultanate of Oman in September, 2000.

While I was excited about the prospects of living in a foreign country, I had my fears too. I wasn't sure if I would have enough people whom I could connect with. What if my colleagues and students at the university looked down on me? What if it was hard for me to be accepted? These are common fears that most immigrants have. However, when I got there, I was pleasantly surprised by the diverse group of students and staff that the college had managed to attract. There were people from different parts of the world, who had come to Oman to enhance their knowledge or explore job prospects in a foreign country. At that time, it was a small campus, and it was only affiliated with Glasgow Caledonian University. However, during my 9 years there; it transformed into one of the Topmost Private Career College in Oman.

A few people there, at the campus, were staff members from Canada, living & working in Oman. I was extremely keen to talk to them about my experience, and how I thought that Canada & Canadians were unfair. I wanted to tell them that Canada didn't know how to value the right people. That's exactly what I did, and to my surprise they patiently listened to me. They weren't offended by my words, but they empathized with me. They appreciated that waiting outdoors for hours on a wintery morning would have been extremely challenging. In fact, one of them went up to the extent of inviting me for lunch. They wanted to introduce me to the 'Canadian Way,' one that I hadn't been introduced to yet. They wanted to show me what real Canada was like.

'Who cares about the Canadian Way?' I thought. However, I had to accept the lunch invitation to return their favour. They had been kind to me, and I couldn't be rude. The lunch was planned at one of the colleague's residence on a weekend. I got a ride there, and here I was at a Canadian colleague's place to know more about the 'Canadian Way.' As soon as I got into my friend's residence, I was presented with the Canadian flag. They told me about Canada, and how the country appreciated & encouraged diversity, more than most other countries in the world. I was educated about how Canadians would go out of their way to make an immigrant feel comforted and welcome.

This flag became integral part of my story – Proudly showing the same flag at one event

They insisted that I gave another try, but I wasn't really interested then. I didn't want to be disrespectful to my colleagues, and told them that I will consider the option. However, I completely ignored everything they had said. Yes; I was impressed by their hospitality and was intrigued by the Canadian way of living, or at least that's what my colleagues called it. This said; there was no real motivation for me to change my decision of never moving to Canada. Oman was treating me really well. I was happy in that country, and I had made some friends that I could completely rely upon. Professionally too; Oman was giving me everything that I could ever ask for. Ever since the outset, I was happy with the position and the pay that I was offered. However, that was just the beginning; and things got much better after. In about a few years, I was promoted to the position of Assistant Lecturer and it did not take me very long to jump to the 'Lecturer' position at the college. My skills were being appreciated, and there was a lot that I was doing at the campus. I was made the Chief Fire Warden of the campus, and also got the opportunity to sit on the Academic Council . There were other programs that I planned and executed for staff members. In short, there was absolutely nothing that gave me a reason to consider moving to any other place.

Life Changes and So Do Your Choices…

During one of the most professionally successful phases of my life, there was a lot that was happening in the background. I got married in the interim, and now I had one more person that I had to care for. After our wedding, my wife had joined me in Oman. This change in my life had brought about a change in options. I wanted to move and settle in a place where I would be a permanent resident, with all the rights. That's what made my wife and I get back to our drawing boards and think of options. We were thinking of moving to Scotland.

Immigration to Scotland was picking up at that time, and there were some great things I had heard about it. On the other hand, Australia was a fantastic country to move to as well. The weather is moderate, and people are known to be inviting. The third option was to reconsider Canada. Despite my hatred for the country because of what had happened to me at the visa office in New Delhi, Canada still was a good option. The country already had a reasonably large Indian diaspora. That will ensure that we don't miss our country all that much. Plus, the option of being a Permanent Resident there would let me raise my family with complete peace of mind, knowing that I had all the rights that any other Canadian had.

With these three options in mind, I started doing my research. In the meantime, I also started looking at application proccooco. Application process for Canada's Federal Skilled Program was pretty simple, and with some help; I got that completed in no time. I sent out the application, and continued to work on my other options in that period. Times for visa processing weren't as short as they are now. It used to take months, if not years, for one to hear back from visa offices. The period can be so long that you are no more nervous, because you aren't thinking about it anymore. You have done your job, and the ball is now in the visa office's court.

My friends used to ask me about the status of my application, and I always told them that I would prefer Scotland or Australia over Canada. However, as fate had it; the first response I got was from Canada. My file number had been generated, and we were now a step closer to being Canadian Permanent Residents. It was a funny feeling. The country that I had hated all this while was opening its doors to me. As much as I was trying to repel anything to do with Canada, it was finding a way to sneak into my life. Be it my Canadian colleagues at the campus or this favorable response to my visa application; it all

9

seemed like destiny was at play. In India; we strongly believe that you only get what's destined for you. It seems that I was made for Canada, and God was adroitly laying a winding road for my journey.

It did take a few more months for my visa file to move to the next steps, but everything fell in place. So, here it was. I was holding a letter from the Canadian visa office. This was reminiscent of that cold day in New Delhi, when that Visa Officer stood in front of me and sealed my fate. This time, though, it was a letter that had delivered the news to me. My visa file was approved, and I was required to send my passport for stamping. After all that had happened in the last few months, I was well past that stage of debating about whether I wanted to give up my dislike for Canada. This was the time for me to act quickly. I consulted my wife, and we were both in agreement that we should send our passports and begin preparing for our move to Canada.

The realization of me moving to Canada took some time to sink in. After it did happen though, I got a little concerned. I was still sure that this was a decision in the right direction, but I was worried about our short-term wellbeing. I was leaving a great position for something I didn't know anything about. Yes, there were a few websites that I visited and read about success stories of immigrants to Canada. In fact, I also spoke with a few of my contacts in Canada. However, it was still like shooting in the dark. There was little that I could change, though. I had to leave it for when I got there. Right now, my wife and I sold off our belongings in Oman and moved to India. We wanted to spend some time with the family before moving to Canada. We also had a daughter now, and we wanted her to spend some time with her grand parents.

Plus, I registered myself and my wife for Canada's Pre-Arrival program in India. Many of my contacts in Canada had talked highly about that program and how it prepared them to understand the country better. So, that was another reason why I had to spend time in India before making the move.

A group photo taken at CIIP - Pre-arrival information session in Chandigarh, India [August 2009]

Getting to Canada…

It was September of 2009, and I was about to land in the country of my dreams. It was a hazy evening, and the airplane was maneuvering around the thick cover of clouds. The move that I always aspired for was now transpiring in real. However, I wasn't really sure if this was the right decision. What my Canadian colleagues told me in Oman did paint a glorious picture of how beautiful, diverse, and welcoming Canada was. I was assured of the opportunities that will be presented to me there. This wasn't 1998, though. This time, I was travelling with my 22 months old daugther. My family's future was at stake, and a wrong decision could spell doom for us. I was well settled in Oman and I had various avenues open in Punjab, India too. I was still ignoring all of that to move to Canada. Was it destiny or was it the universe's plan to help me realize my long held dream? My question was again answered in the 'Canadian Way.'

I had to hire the services of a porter to help me move my 12 plus pieces of baggage. No, I wasn't bringing the whole of Punjab with me in my bags. However, I was scared by experiences of previous immigrants to Canada who didn't find a job right away. So, my luggage was stuffed with biscuits, other non-perishable food items, sleeping bags, etc. If nothing worked out, we could sleep at the airport. Even if we had to book a hotel room, I didn't have to pay for food.

The porter was overwhelmed by the number of bags I had with me, and courteously asked me if I was in Canada for the first time. I told him how I was moving to the country with my family. The porter immediately pulled out his phone from his pocket, and handed it over to me. He asked me to inform my family that I had reached safely. I was blown away by his gesture, but I had to decline his offer as calling to India would be expensive. However, he insisted that I did so while he loaded the bags on his trolley. A small act of kindness goes a long way in signifying what the country stands for. That's what the Porter did that day. An individual represented Canada for me that day, and gave me all the motivation to transition into a new country with confidence.

The Porter was an epitome of the Canadian Way.

All that I have achieved here in Canada has been strongly assisted by the 'Canadian Way.' It is this willingness of the Canadians to help that makes an immigrant feel at ease.

My wife and daughter with 12 plus pieces of luggage with gentleman who offered his services as a porter at Toronto Pearson International airport.

What I have learned from my brief journey in Canada is that people are willing to help. It is you who needs to take the initiative to understand what you need, and ask the right questions. When you ask the right questions, you get answers that take you to the top.

Ambassador Porter Services
P.O. Box 6036 Toronto AMF, Mississauga, ON L5P 1B2
Tel: 416.776.9892

This is the receipt after paying for the porter services (I still hope that one day, I will see this gentleman and thank him)

CHAPTER TWO
FACE YOUR FEARS

"Nothing in life is to be feared. It is only to be understood." —
Marie Curie

I was really apprehensive and fearful about writing this book. *What do I write about? Where do I start? What stories do I narrate?* These were questions that kept me from writing this book for quite a while. However, one day a close friend told me how writing my book was like putting together my speech. The only difference was that my audience couldn't look at me. They had to assimilate the information through my written words. And here I am, reliving my adventurous transition from a young Punjabi lad to a successful Canadian. Meeting my fear in its face has uncovered a new chapter in my life.

You would agree that we all have our set of fears in life. These fears make it difficult for us to achieve the goals that we have set out with. However, as the beautiful quote at the beginning of this chapter suggests; fear is just a state of mind.

All you need to do is understand the situation, and you will realize that there is nothing to be afraid of.

Here's how my interface with fear panned out during my first days in Canada. Like most immigrants to Canada, I had achieved some position in life before I moved in here. By working in my preferred industry for years, I had grown in my career. Hence, I was concerned about whether I will be able to replicate the same level of success in this country. People told me that finding a white-collared job here without previous Canadian experience would be impossible. Not just that; some of my close friends even went to the extent of suggesting that I got rid of my turban and beard in order to look more 'mainstream.' However, before I could test the job market and address that fear of mine; I had to contend with another fear – one that was affecting my prospects in Canada. This was the fear of taking public transit. No, don't start giggling yet. My fear for public transit was really fierce, and I had my reasons for that.

Firstly, the system of public transit is extremely advanced and completely different from the system I had seen in India and Oman. Secondly, my success in my previous countries had ensured that I wasn't required to take the public transit since many years now.

This wasn't something I could avoid, though. My move to Canada had taken a toll on my finances. My pocket was lighter, and some large, inevitable expenses were staring right at me. My wife's aunt lives in Canada, and she was kind enough to host us during our initial few days in the country. However, the time to find a house was closing in. Moreover, it was important to move around in order to look for a job. All of this would be possible if I was mobile, and the public transit was the only method of commuting I had at that juncture.

I continued to avoid taking the public transit until that day when my wife had to finally step in. Several days had passed since my landing in Canada, and my situation refused to change. I was still under some financial burden…..I was still jobless……And, I still couldn't meet many people due to my immobility. I remember how my wife walked up to me that day, and told me about how I was always a winner and had taken all challenges head on. If I managed to get over my worst fear in Canada, I will re-experience the virtue of winning. Despite my resistance to her advice; I knew she was right, and thus decided that it was time to take on my fear. There was nothing to be gained in holing myself up in my house, hoping that some employer would come looking for me. So, I walked out of my house with the intent of riding the bus for the first time in Canada. In the beginning, I kept staring at the road for a while. I could see multiple busses, but I wasn't sure which one to take. Like a meticulous business person, I was evaluating the pros & cons of various possible options. Porter's 5 forces model was pulled out of the hat to evaluate all possible outcomes of taking one bus over the other. After a comprehensive situation analysis, I boiled down to an important question – *'Do I really have to take the bus?'* I would, however, think of going back to my wife without succeeding. That made we want to do it for her. That's when I put my analytical mind to rest, and resorted to some guess work. I decided to board the bus from main terminal at Square One in Mississauga. As soon as I reached at the terminal, I stood close to a random bus stop and decided to board the bus that first arrived , and it happened to be 10-North. I was ahead of the queue of people waiting to board the bus, but I wanted to be kind by letting other people go first. Actually, no. I wanted other people to go so I could know what to do after boarding the bus. Of course, I thought for a second that a bus conductor (assistant found on Indian busses) would walk up to my seat in the bus and ask me where I wanted to go. However, that wasn't exactly the process that people were following out here. They would board the bus, and deposit some change at a junction close to the transit operator. I did the same. As soon as I boarded the bus (after all those people who thought I was extremely courteous to let them go first), I started depositing loonies into that cash box. One, two, three, four..... I didn't know how much to deposit. I was fortunate in that the transit operator held my hand, and said that I had already deposited enough money for the ride.

So, here I was; I had boarded my first Canadian bus. Had I conquered my fear? No; in fact I had aggravated it. The bus was plying on a route I knew nothing about. Was this Mississauga or Bermuda Triangle? It didn't matter as I was lost either way. As we kept moving forward, my heart kept sinking; worrying about the possibilities of getting lost in an unknown country on my very first bus ride. I could even imagine myself being in news the next day – *A tall, stout, and bearded brown man with turban dies of anxiety.* Well, perhaps I am just exaggerating about the news part. I just thought I will die; I didn't think of being in the news. In any case, the situation was getting pretty difficult.

Fortunately, I decided to share my concern with the transit operator who dropped me off right opposite the bus shelter for 10-South- the bus that will take me back. The journey on the way back proceeded as planned, and that concluded my first experience of the Canadian public transit. Walking home from where the bus dropped me off, I had a feeling of accomplishment. I felt that I had managed to conquer the first challenge of my life in Canada, and everything else was going to fall in place. In fact, that small bus ride to-and-from home went a long way in lending me the confidence that was required to meet all my fears head-on.

When you take up any new challenge in life, you will certainly have fear in your mind. You might decide to take the adventure of moving to a new country. On the other hand, you might start your enterprise or start a new job. There are several challenges that you might need to face in your lives, and they will all be loaded with fears and inhibitions. Fighting those fears and inhibitions is what it takes to move closer to success. From all my previous experiences, I have realized that your aim should be to identify your biggest fear that is obstructing your way to success. Once you look at your worst fear in the eye and beat it comprehensively, that is when you will have the conviction to be able to move forward briskly.

Another thing that comes out of this story is the significance of having such people in your lives that are willing to support you in times of disparity and fear. If you have a wife who loves you to death or your parents or friends or other relatives, you feel confident to address all concerns in your life. You know that even when everything goes wrong, you have someone to fall back upon. That's what you call your support system.

Daman (Sukhjit's wife) gives her take on the story:

"I believe that life is all about momentum. Sukhjit has been a winner, and his accomplishments helped him take on new challenges with confidence. However, moving to Canada seemed to have taken him back a little bit. Taking the public transit might seem like a simple task for all of us, but it wasn't for Sukhjit. That was why I had to inspire him to go defeat his fear. If he would have let his fear continue to get the better of him, he would have lost all the momentum that he had gained in India & Oman. I am proud of the way he did it for me, and as I guessed; that day got him the confidence & the momentum he needed to succeed- all over again."

CHAPTER THREE

LEARN; UNLEARN; RELEARN

"The difference between a successful person and others is not a lack of strength, not a lack of knowledge, but rather a lack of will" — Vince Lombardi

J am absolutely sure that many of the immigrants, who are reading this book, would be currently looking for a job. In fact, the word 'Job' is like a keyword that attracts us towards it. Whenever I utter this word in my speeches, people's eyes get wide open and their ears stretch out to extract all the information that I am going to share. While it is funny, it also tells us about this grave issue that most immigrants face- that of finding the right job. We all take some time to get into that evasive 'Right' job. Worse still; many of us don't even manage to get a job for a long-long time. So, what is it that keeps us away from the position that is best suited to our profile and experience? Some say it is the lack of knowledge. Someone would have certainly told you that gathering the desired knowledge is imperative to success in the Canadian job market. However, according to me; it is not all about what you know. It is about educating yourself on what's relevant, and at the same time unlearning all the obsolete information that you have been retaining. You need to get rid of the old baggage that's bogging you down. That's not where it ends. You have to continue to relearn all your logics, and adapt to changes.

When I moved to Canada, I was like most other immigrants – looking for a job. Taking that bus ride to-and-from my home had instilled the confidence in me. I was convinced that I would get a wonderful job, and I had started working seriously towards that. I picked up my resume that I had made in Oman (one that had been sensationally successful there), and tweaked it a little to suit my current scenario. I changed my address, and shortened the resume a little bit (People had told me that Canadians prefer resumes that are shorter than 2 pages). Once that was done, I began making job applications. It started with one job application a day. However, as days passed by; I started applying for more jobs- sometimes even 5 to 7 every day. I had access to some of the online job portals, and I was applying for any job that was in my area. In fact, I started off by focusing on training and marketing as that is where my core skills lie. Going forward, someone suggested that I broaden my purview to be able to kick-start my career (remember those not-so-success immigrants with the mantra to success?). That suggestion resonated with me, and I started looking at some of the administrative positions. The belief was that getting into an administrative role would be easy. When there was absolutely no response with that either, I had to finally budge and apply for warehouse jobs. However, my career was like our world economy these days – GOING NOWHERE.

It had now been a few weeks since I moved to Canada, and absolutely nothing had transpired. My zeal towards making job applications was dying down a little bit with every passing day. How could it be that after making hundreds of job applications, there's not a single person who is interested in my profile. Is it even possible that a profile that was stupendously successful in Oman and India was not even being picked up in Canada? Was it because my name was not 'Mainstream'? Obviously, Sukhjit is not Steve, Sam or Richard, right? All these thoughts hovered my head, and I am absolutely certain that every single immigrant has gone through this phase at some time or the other. However, like the quote at the beginning of this chapter goes; it is not the lack of knowledge or strength that holds us back, it is the lack of will. I say that for a reason, and I will explain that as we go on. At this time, let us get back to my story as things are just about to turn around.

A Job Workshop: My last ditch attempt at finding a job...

After having tried all that I could to land a job and pay for my family's spiraling expenses, I decided that something had to change. If people ever ask me about the turning point of my life in Canada, I tell them that it was the realization that this wasn't India or Oman. What worked there might not work here, and my few weeks of failed attempts at finding a job was a case in point. Hence, I looked at some of the workshops that the federal government organizes for new immigrants. Their popularity could be gauged by the fact that 4 of the 5 places I called for enrollment were fully booked. I was fortunate to find myself a spot in the 5th one. The workshop was about settling into Canada, and it was supposed to touch upon such topics as Canadian culture, weather, navigating around the city, and most importantly: finding a job here. I still remember how it was just the 3rd day into the workshop when I realized that Canada was different. The word 'Networking' came up again and again. It was ridiculous how everyone was talking about the virtues of networking, and I didn't know anything about it.

Building your Network as an Immigrant...

Most attendees of that workshop ridiculed the concept of 'Networking.' "Yes, we know some people here" they would say. "My uncle who does night shifts in a factory, and his wife who works on a contract at a café. Their kids' monthly education fund is being used to buy groceries. Can these people help me get a job in my field?" they will facetiously ask. They were all correct. Immigrants don't have a network that they can use to generate job opportunities. The people that they know are either themselves struggling to make ends meet or are working at a non-so-important position in some firm. Does that mean that it is impossible to break that vicious cycle?

As I walked out of the workshop that day, my mind was working overtime. I couldn't come to terms with the fact that I had absolutely no way of getting myself a job. Yes, recruiters wouldn't have the time to read through every resume they get. Yes, I didn't have a substantial network here in Canada. No, I wasn't willing to accept defeat just like that. I boarded the bus towards home, and that reminded me of how a simple task like boarding the bus was difficult for me, once. Networking is the same thing. If we find the right process and the places to network, perhaps we can build our own base of connections.

Adding 'Will' to my Profile...

Let's come back to the topic of lack of 'will.' All of us quickly realize that sending out mass job applications wouldn't get us anywhere. However, we keep trying to achieve success with this tool. We have the desired knowledge and even the strength, but not the will to accept that we are wrong. We need that will to accept that there is a better way that exists.

After returning home from the 3rd day of my job workshop, I browsed through various Training & Marketing related positions that would suit my profile. I looked at all those job qualifications that were required for the same. Did I have all of the required qualifications? If not, I had to start achieving those through certification courses, volunteering, and more. Moreover, I had to tweak my resume to include specific keywords for different positions. In short, I had to customize my resume to suit the needs of the employer.

As about networking, I had to start creating my own network. The first stage in the process was to go out 'Cold Calling.' I always call it 'Double Cold Calling.' This is because not just can you expect to receive a cold shoulder from the person you meet, you have to also deal with the frantic cold weather of this country.

However, as they say; god has given us the ability to define our own destiny. I had commenced on a journey to build my network, and use that network to carve out a successful career. I used to knock on at least 25 to 30 doors every day around the Square One area in Mississauga. I would walk into an office, and speak with the receptionist about my profile. I would tell them that I was a new immigrant, and wanted to share my profile with prospective recruiters. There were various responses that I generated. Some people were kind enough to introduce me to the company's HR, and that was a way for me to get their business card and add them to my network. Some other times, I was kept away. Either way, I was creating a stir. By the end of the second month, I had gathered a large number of business cards – all of relevant people. These were people who could definitely hire me or refer me to a job. Every now and then, I would call them and remind them that I was still looking for an opportunity.

Where did all this effort lead me? Did it get me the job of my dreams? I shall tell you that as we go on. For now, though, I would like to elucidate the significance of gathering deep knowledge about this country before you begin looking for ways to succeed. You have to understand what this country expects from people and what elements of your personality can help you catch people's attention. One thing that I learned in the process is that Canadians are simple people, and all they are looking for in you is honesty and hard-work. However, the key to using this knowledge constructively is to first unlearn everything you knew from your previous experiences in other countries. Would you go to McDonald's and ask for a Double-Double coffee? You wouldn't because these are different cafes, and what's on offer is different too. Once you open your eyes to the glorious new reality that is in front of you, new avenues will open up and lead you to the path to success. Also, it is imperative that you never cease your process of learning. There's always a new thing you will find out that will promise to make your future even brighter. This not just relates to the job market, but to various other facets of your life too.

Dorothy Maciag-Zwolski (Employment Consultant) gives her take on the story:

"The first impression of Sukhjit came from the very moment when I looked at my new group some years ago and all the participants looked to be a little bit uncertain. However, Sukhjit's face was telling me "I want to learn about everything." Then, I realized I had someone in my group who was willing to learn and assimilate the Canadian way of life.

I knew immediately that such a person was a great asset to the group as this kind of attitude was not that popular among Newcomers.

The day following our first Job Finding Club session proved that he was a pleasure to cooperate with. A very good listener, open minded, listening to all suggestions and advises and most of all willing to follow and eventually change.

During the first mock interview he wore a yellow turban and a very bright shirt, and that made him a very flashy person to be seen from far away. So, I made a comment that looking so flashy covered both lack of skills or experience. He disagreed with me at that moment, but after a few days he came to the conclusion that different cultures have different ideas about how colours are perceived. That, I suppose, was right.

It was his own outcome of the mock interview that proved to me that he was going to adjust to his new country quickly and with ease. I also noticed his sense of humour, which I think is very helpful in smoothly transitioning to the new environment."

CHAPTER FOUR

THEY ARE JUST THE SAME

"Reality exists in the human mind, and nowhere else." –
George Orwell

M y tryst with cold calling had just begun. There were certainly instances where people shooed me away. However, there were many more cases when people were encouraging and willing to support. Obviously, I couldn't expect all of them to have a ready job for me; but they were kind enough to keep my resume on file. In fact, some of them even went to the length of guiding me on my future course of action towards securing a good job.

This experience brought me to another juncture of my journey. It brought me closer to the realization that all humans think and act in absolutely the same way. When I moved as an immigrant, I was made to believe that the people in Canada are not the same as us. We are expected to act differently. I have already told you the 'remove your turban' story, where my close friends and so called well-wishers thought that looking 'mainstream' was important. Many of these friends & well wishers have gone to the extent of trying to speak in Canadian accent, and they suggested I did the same too. However, it is very easy to recognize when you are trying to do something that against your identity and core nature. Canadian accent is not the one that you are brought up with, and faking it truly sounds ridiculous.

I remember an interesting instance when one of my friends came to meet me after I landed in Canada. He walked up to me as if to hug me in perfect Punjabi style. However, he stopped a few steps before that and stretched his arm forward to shake hands with me. If that wasn't shocking enough, he took a deep breath and spoke with the maximum twang he could get in his tone – "How you, pra?" (Just to clarify 'pra' means brother in Punjabi). This was actually the first time I heard someone speak Punjabi in such strange wannabe-western accent.

He continued "How life? Canada nice nice... Good choice (that rhymes...)." It was interesting how he was trying extremely hard to come across as North American, and his attempts were failing miserably.

This, and many similar incidents, had indicated to me that changing one's identity isn't a possibility. You live with what you are. I was hoping that people here would accept me the way I was. My days of cold calling for a job got me an answer for the same. In the initial few days of cold calling, I was extremely conscious about my differences. This had been further accentuated by all those things that I was repeatedly told by my friends and relatives. When I used to walk into office doors, I used to think that people at the reception were gaping at my different appearance. I would think to myself "Would these people make fun of my unusual appearance after I left?"

"Would my long beard and turban be repulsive to people?"

If that difference in appearance wasn't enough, I spoke in my Punjabi-Indian accent. I didn't want to try to speak like Canadians for the risk of sounding like the friend I spoke to you about earlier. However, my existing accent wasn't taking me anywhere either. What would compound the issue was that I would also tend to miss a few things that Canadians would tell me. I remember a few cases when people failed to understand what I said (and vice versa), and that created a funny scene.

One of those instances still makes me laugh. I was at a grocery story. At the cash register, the girl billed us for $47.80 and asked me "How'll ya pay today?"

I was extremely pleased by that, because I thought that this was a great way of helping Canadians balance their expenses. Isn't it wonderful that new immigrants get a choice to pay right now or later? I say that because I actually thought she was saying "Will you pay today?" I answered back saying "No, we wouldn't pay today." As you would expect, the girl at the cash register was taken aback for a second. She recovered herself from the shock of what she had just heard and said "I am sorry, sir. You have to pay." I was lucky that I had a friend with me, who told me about the gross misunderstanding that had happened there. Imagine what would have happened if I insisted that I wouldn't pay 'today.'

At the time of cold calling, I wanted to make sure that such problems wouldn't come up. After all, it was about getting the right job. I would try to speak slowly, and that helped a little. However, there were still cases when people had to courteously ask me to speak in English. Well, that was embarrassing. With the passage of time, I learned to communicate myself better. To be honest, we should say everyone learned over time. While I started speaking slowly, Canadians started understanding Punjabi-Indian accent. That brought us to the same page.

As I continued to call, though, I realized that all we think about, in terms of our differences, is not exactly accurate. I started this chapter with a beautiful quote that says 'Reality lies in the human mind.' Hence, it is important that you sort your mind before you initiate any activity in a new country. What we think can actually make us believe that things exist in a certain manner, but that might not exactly be the truth. The cultural differences that exist between countries make people look & act differently. However, that doesn't mean that we are all different from inside. I believe that beyond the façade of culture and nationality, our inner selves are all the same. We all have 'red' blood running through our veins, and I haven't seen anyone with three legs instead of two. More importantly, we are all made up of values that guide us towards helping people in need and being kind of someone who's trying.

After walking into numerous doors for days and weeks together, I started to find some traction. All those people who had kept my resume on file and ones who had helped me with a reference for another position had lent me the confidence to be myself. They had given me the ability to believe that I could practice my religion by keeping my beard and turban. I could also speak in my unique accent, without being judged for it. However, that had all now started to culminate into opportunities. People here knew that what they needed to judge was not my appearance, but the skills that I presented to their company. As I said, we are all the same. That got me an opportunity that changed my life and helped me meet the real 'me.'

CHAPTER FIVE

DISCOVERING MY TRUE SELF

"If you don't get lost, there's a chance you may never be found." - Anonymous

re you a traveller? Do you like to explore new things? For many people, the ability to discover new horizons is one of the most satisfying feelings. While you traverse new territories, you discover a little more about your true self. As you wander in unchartered terrains and let your senses be amazed by your experiences, you continue to learn about your motivations & inspirations. That's what volunteering can do to your career. It gives you the ability to walk on untraveled paths, and carve out a career for yourself that you are truly passionate about.

When I landed in Canada, I was directionless about my future. I was going about doing things with the hope that something would click someday. A case in point is the variety

31

of job profiles that I was applying for. All I wanted to do was to find a job that would help me pay for my expenses. I was looking for something through which I could afford the basic necessities of life....something with which I could bring back the smile on my daughter's face. That's what we all do, don't we? However, doing something that does not match with your inner-self generally doesn't lead you anywhere. You might even get a job and survive on it, but delivering excellence in doing that is extremely difficult, if not impossible. This reminds me of a popular Bollywood movie (I told you I am a Bollywood fan) in which the lead protagonist rightly puts it *"If Sachin Tendulkar (one of the most successful cricket players in the World) was a singer, would he still be successful?"*

Like many other successful immigrant stories, I discovered my true self and my path to success through Volunteering. The word 'Volunteering' isn't a very popular one back-home. I talk to immigrants from various different parts of the world, and many of them aren't necessarily conversant with this term. They apply selective listening, and only focus on the word 'Work' when I say Volunteer Work.

"I am up for any kind of work, sir. Being new to Canada, I know I have to start somewhere. In fact, I can even customize my resume & cover-letter to make myself worthy of an interview. Can you please tell more about the position?"

The excitement in their tone gets subdued to an extent when I tell them that it is an unpaid position.

"I would love to help the society, but this is time for me to help myself. I promise that I will contribute to this country in any way possible once I am settled. At this time, my family expects me to earn them their daily bread."

My father always tells me that everything in life is about perspective. One way of looking at Volunteer Work is to say that you contribute to the society. Of course, when you are not in a position to make ends meet for your family; helping others is the last thing on your priority list. However, what if I was to tell you that Volunteerism isn't just about helping others; in fact, it is about helping yourself. Not only is it a pathway towards gaining valuable on-the-job experience, it is also a perfect route for you to recognize yourself. It offers you the luxury to try different profiles and identify that one that you absolutely love. After having performed a job we thought we loved back home, volunteering might give us the chance to recognize something else that we are unbelievably passionate about. Let me elaborate upon that with my story.

A few weeks had passed since I had landed in Canada. As you know already, things weren't exactly rosy. I had serious trouble making myself conversant with riding a bus. If that wasn't enough, all my online job applications weren't even garnering an interview call for me. Door knocking had certainly instilled a new-found confidence in me and I had started building contacts, but every passing day was adding significantly to my desperation.

One of my friends introduced me to a website where open volunteer positions were posted. When I visited the site, I was surprised to see the large number of open positions around the area. I could never imagine that there are so many available volunteer positions in GTA and Peel Region in particular. Among those numerous open positions; there was one that suited my profile, but my reaction to it was similar to how most immigrants react to something like this. *"At this stage of life, why would I work for free?"* A few weeks in Canada had, however, taught me to not dismiss an idea without giving it a thought. I started asking some of my friends about whether volunteering would do me any good. My objective was to find out if volunteering could be a path-way to another job. Many of the friends I asked, though, did not respond positively to the idea. Most of them suggested that they had volunteered in the early part of their stay in Canada, and it had apparently not generated the returns they were expecting. However, I wasn't convinced with this explanation. If so many people always talk about the virtues of volunteering, it has to have some value. Being from the field of computing, I know that there are various functions & short-cuts in computer that can be really helpful in performing day-to-day tasks. However, most people don't know how to best use those functions. That's why they never realize the real benefit of the same. That is how volunteering is. It can be your pathway to building those connections and network that you always strive for.

With nothing in hand any way (with regards to job opportunities), I was determined to give volunteerism a try (Beggars can't be choosers, right?). There was an open position for 'Computer Facilitator' at the local employment resource center at YMCA. This was right down my ally, and I was thinking that this can be the gateway for me to prove my worth in the field. I applied for the position, and here I was in my first interview in Canada. Travelling up to the interview location, I was extremely confident. *"Who else would want to offer such a skilled service for absolutely no cost?"* However, to my surprise- the interview room was filled up with candidates. There were so many people who were willing to render their highly skilled service for free. That hinted towards the fact that there were many people who thought volunteering could be a good idea. Of course, the competition made me nervous; but, I knew that I had the skills to get the position. That's exactly how it panned out. I was brilliant in the interview, and the position was now mine. This small success worked wonders for me. For a moment, I stopped thinking about whether it was a good decision to leave a comfortable life in Oman. During this time, I wasn't worried about how I would fund my family's expenses without a proper job. All I was focusing on was to do well at that position as a volunteer.

Life had taken a more beautiful twist as I had a reason to get off my bed every morning. I would apply for jobs in the morning, and teach basics of computers in the evening. During these classes, I met with people from different walks of life. Many of them didn't have any clue about computers. Many others wanted to learn it to advance in their career. It was a feeling of contentment to help people achieve their goals. In fact, that made me work hard to make sure that I was doing what was required to help them in their respective endeavors. Suddenly, this wasn't just about performing a job. This was about going way beyond my job role in order to be of any help to my students, ones who did not have basic computer proficiency. I would feel wonderful when I would manage to convincingly answer my students' questions or be able to add real value to their profile. I would go tell my wife and daughter about how so many of my students thought that I had made a real difference in their lives. This was when things started to change.

This experience had done a couple of things to me. Firstly, it appended the much-desired Canadian experience to my profile. For all those people who were skeptical about hiring me because of the lack of Canadian experience, their objection was now successfully addressed. Secondly, this experience was bringing me closer to my real passion. It was helping me explore another side of my personality- that of a facilitator. For all those of you who haven't ever had an opportunity to share your knowledge with others, you should try doing it once. Conduct a workshop or write a blog or simply organize training at your company; you would realize how valuable it is to contribute to the larger goal. As a new Canadian newcomer, I wanted to contribute to this country like no one else had. I was dreaming of a world where no new Canadian had to struggle to take a bus ride. I was fancying a Canada where people could arrive and develop a step-by-step process towards accomplishing their dreams. The non-profit sector was to offer those opportunities to me, and my work at YMCA was helping me inch closer to such opportunities.

With this understanding with me, I was now ready to look for opportunities in my field. I applied at a few positions, some volunteer some not. It didn't take me long to connect with a non-profit organization in Mississauga. The organization was looking for someone to develop a database for the management of information related to its volunteers. I was so excited about this position (again, this was a perfect fit with my prior experience) that I promptly grabbed the opportunity and even developed a mock-database for the interviewers to see. The Volunteer Co-ordinator at that organization was pleased with my efforts, and even shared the mock-database with the HR Manager, Operations Manager, and the Executive Director. Again, I was doing what I did best- using my knowledge of computers. However, this knowledge was now being utilized to serve my passion.

I wouldn't really like to present a false picture to you at this point. Most of you reading this might think that you don't have the time to volunteer for that long before landing a paid job. Of course, I was in the same boat. I was like any other immigrant. While I was enjoying my role as a volunteer, getting a job was at the back of my mind all the time. I couldn't keep myself away from thinking about my daughter who couldn't buy everything that her friends had. My wife never uttered a word, but I knew she wanted to go for weekly family outings too. I keep coming back to it, but it's so relevant to every immigrant. After having lived a financially comfortable life for years, suddenly holding back on some of the most basic expenses can be extremely challenging. Hence, I was nervous; but I was trying to keep my desperation away for some time. I knew that things had started rolling and it was a matter of time. You have to think of it like a process. If you do all the right things, you will take about 2 months to establish the right contacts. After that, you might have to volunteer for a few more months before you land a great job for yourself. If you know that you have to keep say 4 months as buffer, your mind would be trained to stay calm during that period. That's what happened with me. I stayed strong and continued to deliver unrivalled performance.

After having done some good work as a volunteer, this organization offered me the position of 'Project Assistant.' This was a contract position, and YES- a paid (Honorarium) one this time. All my efforts had reaped the desired returns, and here was my first paid (Honorarium) position in Canada. I was back in the game. More importantly, I could now let my wife have her weekly outings and my daughter buy some of the things that she wanted to.

Volunteering had done the job for me. It had got the ball rolling, but this was just a contract position. More needed to be done. For now, though, it was time to celebrate and prepare to begin a new chapter in my story.

Sweety Khanija (Volunteer Services Coordinator at the organization where Sukhjit got the 'Project Assistant' position) gives her take on the story:

"When I first spoke to Sukhjit he appeared to be a very hardworking individual and someone who would be able to bring many practical and technical skills which would benefit the organization. Sukhjit was looking for opportunities to where he could put his foot in as a new comer and explore the possibilities of utilizing his educational background and work experience. He has had a major impact on the organization where he has helped build a volunteer database. The purpose of the database was to help us track the volunteers coming in and the work that was being done.

Overtime Sukhjit built a strong relationship with members and staff. I can truly say that Sukhjit has overcome many obstacles as a newcomer to Canada, and I have seen his development over time."

CHAPTER SIX

FIRED BEFORE BEING HIRED

"Sometimes life gives you a second chance because just maybe the first time you weren't ready." – Unknown

So, I told you in the previous story of how I had got a paid position on the basis of my volunteering work. My confidence was kissing the sky, and I was ready to make some serious advancement in my career. However, there was a brief period just before that time when things seemed like they weren't falling in place. This was the time from when I started volunteering to when I finally got my 'Project Assistant' job. All the job applications that I was making weren't reaping any benefit. I would receive some interviews, but they would not be the desired profile. For all the other applications, I wouldn't hear back from the recruiters.

I remember that day when I was chatting with my wife in the evening. Amidst all the distress in life, those 30 minutes of chat with my wife every evening was something that we both looked forward to. Returning home after a hard day out in the field, I would find a great companion in my wife. I would share all the stories and the hardships I was facing in the process. She's a friend who understands me, and gives me the confidence to get off the bed the next day and get to work. That day wasn't any different. I had just returned home after meeting about 15 to 20 companies. Many of them had accepted my resume, but I didn't see anything meaningful coming my way any time soon. Something had to give. As you know, at that time I was working on 2 volunteer positions. While volunteering gave me great satisfaction, it wasn't helping me put food on the table. My wife suggested to me that I spoke with a few of our relatives and friends who had gone through the same phase in life. I thought it was a good idea; and without wasting much time, I started browsing through my phone book to see who could be spoken with. There were a couple of people whom I thought could shed some light on what needs to be done for an instant job that could pay for our expenses. I was absolutely willing to do anything that I needed to do. So, I called both of them right away.

Surprisingly, both people I spoke with, suggested that what I was doing (physically calling-on and networking-with companies) wasn't going to help. They were of the opinion that the most suited profile for any immigrant was one at a warehouse. To make it clear, what they were talking about was being a worker at a factory. They thought that no one in Canada cared about the immigrants' profile, experience, or prowess. Hence, being at the warehouse was where everyone had to start. At first, I was extremely apprehensive about what was being said to me. With my computer knowledge, degree and rich experience, I couldn't work in a warehouse. It will be strange for me to be lifting heavy packages and parcels, especially given the fact that I had always worked in an office setting. My shoulders were used to lifting the weight of my recruiters' high expectations, but they were not necessarily heavy packages. Think of my age too. I had been through the initial rigors of my career, and had grown beyond that. Thinking of taking up a temporary factory worker position was quite a plunge.

However, what my contacts said was compelling too. They said that my expenses were spiraling, and unless I had a job very soon; it will get difficult for me to manage. A few more months like this could even push me towards bankruptcy. Of course, that was correct. They were also right in their opinion that getting a factory position might be easier than landing myself a job in my field. I knew that my ideal job position would require me to go through multiple interviews, and that will be time consuming.

While my wife wasn't really convinced with me losing hope and taking up a position that didn't fit my scheme of things, I was determined that I at least wanted to have something temporarily to pay for my family expenses. One of the two contacts I spoke with that day shared the contact information of a recruitment agency with me. He had worked with that agency before, and was of the opinion that they could arrange something promptly. That sounded good, and I decided to give the agency a call the next day.

As sun rose over the horizon the next morning, I woke up with determination. My wife sat next to me and ensured that I was not making a brazen decision. She was supportive as always, and said that the family could survive frugally until I had the desired job. I didn't have to do something that I never wanted to do, just for the sake of my family. In fact, my wife was willing to look for some work herself; if we could have someone look after my young daughter. It wasn't feasible to pay someone to sit my daughter while we both looked for work. How would we manage to pay for that expense? At the same time, living frugally was something we were already doing. As I said earlier, being without a job for another few weeks could slide our family into great financial difficulty. Hence, I decided to go ahead and make the call to the recruitment agency. With all the calling and networking I had done in the last couple of months, I was confident about my ability to strike a conversation. I called up the recruitment agency, and the call was received by a pleasant, female voice.

"How can I help you?" she asked.

I answered with purpose *"One of my friends was placed at a factory through you. I am looking for a similar job and want to know if you can help."*

She had some pleasant news for me *"You look like a good candidate. We have an urgent opening with one of our clients. Are you going to be available tomorrow?"*

This was good. I was thrilled that there was something that I could start with the next day itself. There was no time to waste. I quickly accepted the offer, and confirmed the location. While I had never been to that place before, I was pretty sure I could make it there on time.

She thanked me for my promptness and asked me *"Do you have hard toed shoes?"*

People had told me about the virtue of hard-toed shoes. I knew that every factory job would require me to possess a pair of those. Hence, I answered in the affirmative. As soon as I kept the phone down, I shared the good news with my wife. She continued to support me; but deep within, she knew that this wasn't what I was here to do. Anyway, she encouraged me and I left immediately after to get the coveted hard toed boots. I had never seen such shoes before; obviously, because I was never required to be in a factory before. Walking into Walmart, I was feeling as if all my education was good for nothing as all I could get for myself was a factory position and a pair of hard toed shoes. I needed to focus on the present, though. It was imperative for me to get the right shoes so they were comfortable when I worked. I asked one of representatives there about the same, and she directed me to the correct aisle. There seemed to be multiple shoes there, all of varied quality. It didn't make sense to invest a lot in a shoe, but my safety was important too. Thus, I decided to buy the quality that wasn't the cheapest, but wasn't very expensive either. I felt troubled paying $80 for those shoes, but who knew that this was going to turn out to be the most valuable possession of my life?

The next day of my life was pretty interesting. I was nervous and excited at the same time. Today, I was going to make some money for myself and my family. It was my first official day of paid work in Canada. Plans were being formed in my head about how I was going to use that money. First and foremost, I wanted to buy something nice for both my wife and my daughter. They had been devoid of all the luxuries that they were used to in Oman. I could at least get some part of it back for them. The rest of the money could be used to buy some groceries that we had been holding back on.

My wife got up early that day and made me a wholesome lunch. I was going to need that, given that it was going to be a long and laborious day for me. I packed my lunch and hard-toed shoes in my backpack, and walked out to take the transit. My wife brightened the morning with her smile and wished me luck.

I think that women are way stronger than men. My wife was being required to go through this, but could not show any sign of disappointment or sorrow. She had to keep my spirits up and also ensure that our daughter was never affected by any of this. She could easily decide to look for work, and thrust all household responsibilities to me. However, she knew that our daughter needed her mother more than her father. So, she willingly put aside her ambitions for the time-being for the sake of her family. Could I have ever done that? Perhaps not!

So here I was, travelling towards my first factory position in life. As mentioned earlier, I had mixed feelings about this. Yes, money was an important factor; but, I wasn't sure if I was getting into the right thing. I didn't want this to consume all my time, and make it difficult for me to look for other jobs. Consumed in my thoughts, I didn't realize how quickly I reached my destination. I got down at the stop and started looking around for the place that I had to go to. According to my internet research, the place was supposed to be on the right hand side of the bus stop. I kept looking in that direction, but I couldn't see anything. There were some buildings, but their names were covered by large trees on that road.

The road was busy as it was close to the peak office hour. When I couldn't really ensure which building was I supposed to go to, I decided to start walking. I went up to the pedestrian crossing, and waited for my light. There were 23 more seconds before the other side's light would turn red. Those 23 seconds, however, felt more like 23 minutes. My heart was pounding and sweat was rolling down my forehead. I was obviously nervous. While I wasn't really late, I was still anxious about getting to my destination quickly. There was a lot of uncertainty about the work I was supposed to perform today; so, I wanted to start my day as soon as possible. You must know that uncomfortable feeling, when your mind is consumed with fear and strange thoughts cloud your perspective.

I walked towards those buildings I could see from the other side of the road, and realized that the first building wasn't the one I was looking for. I continued to walk, and the next few buildings weren't the ones either. Wait a minute! The address on those buildings didn't seem right. It was the same street where I had to be, but the unit numbers were far off from what I was looking for.

My heart started pacing a little now. I had done my research, and it was supposed to be around where I was standing then. My palms became sweaty, and I wasn't sure if calling the recruitment agency was going to be a good idea. There wasn't a choice I was left with, though. I got my phone out and called the agency. It was the same sweet voice that had offered me this opportunity the previous day.

"This is Sukhjit. I had spoken with you yesterday about a job. I am at the location right now, but I can't see the office around...."

She cut me short right there and literally screamed at me. *"That's the very reason why we don't want to help newcomers. They always create problems. You know how important this client is for us? We trusted you, and now you are acting irresponsible."*

Perhaps, she was thinking that I was lying to her. They would be used to no-shows from candidates. However, she had to know that I was not being irresponsible. She had to know that I was genuinely lost.

45

I responded back saying *"I understand what you are saying, ma'am. However, I am not being irresponsible. I have arrived at the location on time, but I can genuinely not find the place. If I was to do a no-show or something, I would never call you; would I?"*

That mellowed her down a little and she asked me *"What intersection are you at?"*

Our conversation beyond that time was way too embarrassing for me to share here. All that you need to know is that I was at the wrong intersection. How could that happen, you would think. That's what I thought to myself too. I had travelled Mississauga & Brampton enough by then for me to not get to the wrong destination. However, this had happened now and I wasn't sure what next.

"It is a mistake, ma'am. Give me 20 minutes, and I will be at the right location." I said.

However, she was in no mood to budge. She did all she could to insult me to the core. I was made to believe that I was good for nothing. After yelling at me for a few minutes, she said *"You are fired."*

I couldn't believe what I was being told. *"Ma'am, it's just a matter of 20 minutes. I will get to the location and start working immediately. Moreover, I can work longer in the evening to cover for the delay."* That's all I could manage to say in order to make her not fire me.

However, she said her decision was irrevocable and I was left stranded in the middle of nowhere with my lunch and pair of hard-toed shoes. I was fired even before being officially hired. I was thinking to myself as to why would I be subjected to such misfortune. However, I would like to refer to the quote that I have shared at the beginning of this story. Looking back at that incident today, I think that life gave me a second chance by getting me fired even before being hired. Had I got into that factory that day; perhaps, I wouldn't have managed to achieve the success I did. The fact that I did got fired allowed me to focus on my job-search and land myself a great job.

I said earlier that those hard-toed shoes became my most valuable possession. The reason was that I decided to use them as inspiration. Every time I look at those shoes, I get reminded of what I had to go through to achieve what I have today. I had to be yelled at. I had to be fired for the first and the only time in my life. All of that makes me respect my present and work harder to retain it.

What I also learned that day was that you can attract or repel things. Our family always tells us about the virtues of staying positive. My wife strongly believes in that. That reflects in how she always comforted me during those days of struggle. She had made me lunch that morning and kept me motivated. After having lost my job (even before having it), I didn't have the fear of being judged by her. I knew that I could go back home, and pour my heart out to her. She will have a smile on her face throughout the conversation, and will tell me that it's okay. She believes that there's something better that is always waiting for us. That's why I still get goose bumps when I think of what happened that day. I am not talking about being fired from that position, but about the phone call that I received on my way back. This was a phone call that was going to change my perspective about life. Remember, I told you about the 'Project Assistant' position I got offered from one of the not-for-profit organizations I was volunteering for? I got it on that very day, when I was heading back home. I got a call and they asked me to start immediately. During times of despair, there is one moment of luck that makes you realize that God does exist. There is an almighty that is looking after you.

CHAPTER SEVEN

THE ANATOMY OF DIVERSITY

"Culture is the widening of the mind and of the spirit." – *Jawaharlal Nehru*

here are times in life when things don't go as planned. It is at this very moment that we lose hope. As an immigrant, each one of us goes through such volatile moments. When you are starting a new life, there is so much to know that it can take years for you to gather all of that. Every new thing might pose as a roadblock, and can threaten to halt your progress. I, however, believe that your wheel of success can slow down but it can never come to a complete halt. As long as you are confident about your abilities and are willing to put in the hard work, things will continue to work out for you. In fact, many people believe that hard times can make you learn more than the good times do.

Picking up from where we left in the last chapter, I was still volunteering at 2 places. One of these volunteer positions had now turned into a paid(Honorarium) contract position. So, things were getting slightly better. I had spent the last few days celebrating with my family and friends. Although I was not going to be rich doing what I was doing, but things had at least started moving in the right direction. There was more work that needed to be done. With my confidence kissing the sky, I had started adopting unique & innovative ideas to improving my life in Canada. I was making complete use of the only 2 free things that you can find in this country. The first among them was the ability to talk to people. I would take the bus to work every day and run into different kinds of people. Many of these people were senior citizens, who had either moved to Canada years ago or were parents of the immigrants- visiting their kids. I would chat away with these senior citizens in the bus, and gain knowledge about life. By the virtue of their age, they knew much more than I did. Additionally, talking to people also helped me expand my network. It was not just the lack of job that was a problem for me (or most immigrants, in that case), it was the social void that I was experiencing. As a family, we didn't have a social network for us to spend time with, to celebrate our happiness with, and share our sorrows with. These conversations in the bus would help me fill that void. Many times, we would exchange contact information at the end of the conversation and promise to connect again soon. That was certainly going a long way in creating a support system that every person needs.

The second free thing that I would use quite prominently was newspapers and magazines that you find around bus stands and subway stations. You would think, staying updated with the news is a good idea. It definitely is. By knowing what's happening around the world, you develop topics of conversation. When you are in an important meeting or while cold calling, you can use these to your advantage. I will share an interesting instance with you about how being updated regarding what's happening around us helps.

I walked into an office while cold calling, and this is how it panned out:

"Hi, how are you? My name is Sukhjit?"

The receptionist looked back at me. She looked like one of those people who would not really want to help me much. There was not a trace of smile on her face, and she tersely responded *"I am well. How can I help you?"*

My general response would have been 'I am Sukhjit. I have 9 years of experience in teaching computer engineering subjects . I would like to share my resume with you and see if there are any job openings where I can contribute with my qualifications and past experience.'

That was not going to work with her. She would have quickly taken my resume, and asked me to leave. In such situations, you can be pretty sure that the resume would be garbaged right after you leave. Hence, I changed the track of conversation and said *"Thanks for offering your help. Before I start, though, I would like to congratulate you. Blue Jays won again yesterday. Isn't it wonderful?"*

To my luck, she was a baseball fan and her expressions quickly transformed. She responded back saying *"I know. Weren't they awesome? My husband and my son had almost lost hope, but what a superb come back!"*

The conversation was now a little warmer, and that's how I gradually got back to the topic *"I know. Even the experts believe that it was an exceptional come back from Jays. On that positive note, let me get to the topic. I am a computer engineer with teaching experience, looking for a job in my field. Would you be kind enough to introduce me to the HR here so I can pass on my resume and explore possible opportunities in your organization?"*

She did introduce me to the HR manger, and I passed on my resume to him. While this call didn't lead to a real job, it certainly increased my chances of getting one. For all those immigrants trying to expand their network and wanting to develop topics of conversation with Canadians, staying on top of the news is a good idea.

However, building my knowledge is only one reason why I used newspapers and magazines. The other objective was to flip through the pages of these magazines to see if there was anything in there that could help me. There were job advertisements in newspapers. Additionally, there were articles in both newspapers and magazines about being more job-worthy. The more you learn, the more you improve your chances of success. That's the approach I used, and I wouldn't mind reading about things I knew already; hoping that there might be something new that might help me grow my career further. One day, I came across this magazine called 'Canadian Immigrant.' I had never read that magazine before, and trying it out was certainly what I wanted to do. The magazine contained important information about successfully immigrating to Canada. However, one section of that magazine that caught my gaze was the 'Will You Hire Me?' section. Basically, that contained the profile of a few individuals for recruiters to consider. I was immediately impressed by the concept. How wonderful would it be for your profile to reach out to thousands of people in one go? Not only would it make you popular, it will also mean that some recruiter might pick it up and say "That's the kind of guy I was looking for."

The curios person that I am, I decided to write to the editor of the magazine in order to seek the opportunity of having my profile up there. Obviously, I wasn't expecting a response. There are so many immigrants, and not everyone gets a chance to feature in a magazine. However, I was wrong. There was an instant response to my email, and I was asked for details about my profile. What an incredible feeling that was. I was spending a huge amount of time on getting those usual things – job, money to buy gifts for my family, etc. However, it is those unexpected small achievements along the way that make the journey memorable.

So, I was now assigned with the task of sending more details about my profile to the magazine. It was not the usual information that I had on my resume. I had to, instead, think profoundly about myself and my career goal in order to get this right. I had to draw up a Vision statement for my profile. 'Where do I see myself in the next 5 to 10 years?' was the question that I had to ask myself. With so much uncertainty at that stage of my life, I wasn't exactly sure of what my answer to that question was. However, I thought of how I would have expected my life to be in 5 years had I not been facing challenges with immigration. My volunteering experience too had appended a newfound understanding of my personality, and that assisted in the process as well.

Although this took me a very long time to put together, I thought that it was an incredible experience. It helped me be crystal clear of where I wanted to take my career and my life. Once that was clear, the steps towards that vision become more visible. Let us step back and assume that you had to think of a vision for your career and create a step by step guide to getting there. How would you plan that? Use the next couple of pages here for notes and thoughts. Please continuously remind yourself to be honest. If you are struggling to find an entry-level job, your first step can't be to be the manager in a reputed company. You need to find a practical starting point and create a growth plan to reach your goal.

Here's what my vision statement looked like

> *My Canadian career dream is*
>
> *To be a role model/success story for the other new immigrants who are coming from various parts of the world*

I don't know if it is what you thought it would be, but that was the best I could come up with at that time.

After having completed my profile, I sent it back to the editor of the magazine and my profile was now scheduled to be covered in the 'Will You Hire Me?' section in March, 2010.

Thinking back of that day when my profile was supposed to be published in that magazine; I was thoroughly excited. After weeks of cold calling, I had realized that it takes time & effort to build connections. However, this magazine was going to make me reach out to thousands in one-go. Again, I wasn't exactly sure of the kind of response I would receive. By then, I hadn't gauged how popular that magazine was. I did get more sense of the magazine's popularity, though, when I started hearing from people right from the day when my profile was published. The magazine was certainly very popular, and people used to read it. There were many people who wrote back to me wishing me luck in my job search. In fact, there were a few job openings that were shared with me. Out of those, three positions related to my past experience. I was scheduled to meet the concerned people in the coming weeks. In this mix of emails, there was one that was different.

I remember how enthusiastic I was that day after receiving such a heartening response to my profile in the magazine. I was telling my wife about all those people who had wished me luck and those 3 people who were scheduled to meet me in the coming days. We had just about completed dinner, and my daughter was ready to doze off. My wife escorted her to the bed-room, and I decided to check my email one more time before going to bed. I pulled my laptop out and logged into my email. There was 1 unread email, and I opened it with eagerness. As I read the first few words of that email; I knew this wasn't exactly like the other emails I had got over the past few days. By the time I completed reading it all, I was slightly numb. My hands & feet were sweaty and extremely cold. There was a strong burning sensation in my ears and they were so red that my wife could notice immediately. My eyes were wet and my head started hurting. I had been speaking about 'The Canadian Way' to everyone, but here was an anti-example of that. Canada takes pride in its diversity, but this email certainly didn't represent that. I don't think I am a capable-enough writer to describe that email to you. Hence, I have pasted the entire thing for you below:

Hi man!

You find it difficult to find a job primarily because of your anti-western appearance. Canada is not India,man. Not even close. Stop wearing turban in public and shave clean. Man it is not Asia here, get more westernised and you'll be hired shortly after you change yourself into a western person. Canada is not a place to demonstrate identities in extreme forms.

P/S/ And one more thing- your email adress, it's sucha pain in the neck to type it, too difficult and troublesome for an english-speaking person.

Good luck man

I had this strong urge to write back to that person. He had to hear back from me. However, I was fortunate that my wife arrived there and asked me why my ears were so red and my eyes wattery. I responded back to her saying that I was extremely tired, and insisted that we slept. Obviously, I didn't want my wife to know about it. This is because I didn't want her to be exposed to such conduct. Moreover, I was her hero. I was scared that reading these views about me might change that. I wouldn't anymore be that hero who's simply the best in what he does.

I closed my eyes, but my mind was trying to visualize that person who would have written this to me. You might all be thinking why I took it so seriously. The reason is that a new immigrant is short of a support system, and any hit on your conscience tears apart your emotional fabric. Someone was talking about my right to practice my religion without impacting my job prospects, and this wasn't acceptable.

I wanted to go to my laptop and write back to that person, but I didn't do it for the risk of disturbing my wife & my daughter. I tried restraining myself, but I couldn't hold myself anymore. My daughter and my wife were deep asleep, and I slowly stepped out of the bed. I went to my laptop. What to write was the next dilemma. I wanted to give that person a piece of my mind. However, there was nothing I could think of at that point of time. I typed something and deleted it and then typed something again. At the end of the process, all I said there was that I was employed already, and I wasn't sure if he was shocked hearing that. I wished him luck, and advised him to broaden his perspective in life.

Writing that email, no matter how short, made me feel better. I got a good night's sleep, and the bright blue skies next day made my mind start working more logically. I didn't have to be like the other person and start stereotyping. One bad apple can't indicate the quality of the bunch. There was no way I could let that example distort my understanding of Canada and its people. I had to simply move on.

However, that incident certainly told me that I was different from the rest. This could be a disadvantage as was suggested in that email. However, it could also work to my benefit. My different appearance can help people remember me. The more they would think about me, the higher would be my chances of getting a job. Moreover, there was absolutely no way I could change my skin tone or my accent or even my appearance. Hence, I forgot about that incident and moved forward. My focus was now shifted towards using my identity as a vantage point. I would get a job, and I will get it by being myself.

I started this story with a beautiful quote. Culture certainly widens your mind and soul. The one that narrows your thinking is approach. My culture was to be kind to everyone, and continue doing the good work. What had happened had left me hurt, but also more educated. I was more educated about the world that awaits us outside our home. This world is made up of different people, and expecting the same response from everyone is like believing that every player scores a goal in a soccer game.

With my good work and persistence, I expanded my network of friends and well-wishers. These people would help me with job openings that were in my field. In fact, some would even offer references to strengthen my profile for the position. Among all of these positions, there was one that I was thoroughly excited about. It was for being a Settlement Worker in a Not-for-Profit sector. After all I had gone through and what I had learned from volunteering, this position was what I would love to take up. My profile was perfectly suited for the position too, and I felt a very strong urge to want to do it. I had an interview scheduled with the manager there, and I performed the ritual I had developed for interviews. I went to see the place a day in advance. Now, I was conversant with the area and also the bus route. Additionally, I knew how long it will take me to get there comfortably in time. I made sure that I had with me the most recent copy of my resume and a copy of my profile in the 'Canadian Immigrant' magazine. All the positivity that I had managed to bring in me helped and I ensured that my interview was exceptional. They were looking for a person with multi-lingual skills and I could offer that to them. In fact, they even asked me to translate a piece of English literature into Punjabi. They (and even me) were surprised how accurate my translation was. The interview committee was confident that I could perform the job with prowess. However, the interview came to a close with the usual statement – "We will let you know." I was now exhausted of hearing that statement from interviewers. They will be impressed in the interview, but then never call me back. So, I asked them if they had seen my profile in the magazine. This was a gamble I had played to get more time with the committee.

"What magazine?" They looked disinterested and they were clearly trying to shrug me away. However, my profile in a popular Canadian magazine was an achievement wasn't

something I will let them miss. I pulled out the magazine and flipped it open to the page where my profile was.

"There are numerous new immigrants who come to this country every day, every hour. How many of those people manage to have themselves covered in this magazine? How much does it tell you about me and my capabilities?" I said.

This seemed to be the turning point. The magazine was actually a regular at their location, and they also had a copy of it. That seemed to have worked in my favour. They looked at the profile and then looked at each other. *"It seems you truly are extremely competent and passionate.* What you have achieved is something very few people manage to do. The panel members told me that they will soon let me know and will get back to me as soon as possible. The good news came shortly after that.

Yes, this was a job offer. I was on my way to my first formal, full-time position. There wasn't a question of thinking twice. I accepted the position and joined them immediately. I had taken a significant step in my life, but the thought of that hate email was still lingering. However, this time I wasn't thinking about how hurt I was. Instead, I was happy that I used that as a platform to grow into something bigger in life. My positivity and confidence helped me get over an obstacle that threatened to halt my progress in Canada. One email can't suggest that everyone thinks the same. As long as you are good, people would want to work with you. With that thought in mind, I managed to get my first job and move an inch closer towards the unprecedented success that awaited me.

CHAPTER EIGHT

PASSION TAKES YOU PLACES

"If you're not making someone else's life better, you're wasting your time" – Will Smith

hings, as you know, don't remain the same forever. If you are going through a rough phase, you are pretty sure that times would change. Your efforts and passion can further help you catalyze that change in your life. I consider my story to be an interesting illustration of how doing the right things can promptly get you what you have always desired. In hindsight, I believe that it was my passion towards doing everything I did that led me to the path of success. If I had done all the same things, but this time without much passion and purpose, I would have perhaps not succeeded. That's what most of us do, don't we? We find a job and just perform our role. Have we ever tried to think of how we can do our job better? The ones who think about that go a long distance.

I have a close friend who used to be really fat. His brother would force him to work-out so that he could lose weight. However, that work-out never reaped any results for him. One day, the girl of his dreams ridiculed him publicly for being fat and ugly. Can you believe what happened next? He lost 30 kgs in a span of less than 6 months. That was because he was now passionate. He didn't want to look fat in front of the girl he always dreamt of. This is a real story of a friend I have met multiple times. The only strange part of it is that he fell in love with someone else in the process, and is happily married today. Isn't youth a strange-strange time of our lives?

Anyway, coming back to my story - As you know, things had improved considerably in the recent times. I had used my door knocking and volunteering to find myself a job. I was required to work as a settlement worker in the not-for-profit sector. This aligned well with my voluntary experience. More importantly, this experience also coincided with my passion. After having gone through all the rigors of settling into Canada, I had developed this desire to guide my fellow immigrants. I wanted to help these people be prepared and knowledgeable of the road that lied ahead of them. Obviously, walking through that bumpy road is the only way they could succeed. My current job helped me communicate all of this with new immigrants.

My job as a settlement worker would let me be of help and also be exposed to numerous stories of distress, struggle, depression, and even triumph. Now that this was my first formal full-time position and the fact that I loved what I was doing, I wanted to ensure that I was doing it with precision. Towards that cause, I would regularly ask for guidance and feedback from my co-workers and bosses. They had been in this industry for a while now, and they knew what it takes to succeed here. Obviously, all my previous job experience was coming in handy too. While my previous jobs didn't relate with what I was doing now, I could at least draw some learning about professional conduct and more from my prior experience. In short, I was doing all that I could to perform my job better and that was certainly showing positive results.

However, this isn't exactly what I want to tell you about in this story. I want to shed some light on the importance of doing your job better than you are expected to. Like we know - once you find a good job after all the rigors, you are obviously expected to work hard. The only difference was that I was working hard because I was extremely passionate about settlement of new immigrants. That passion took me to an interesting twist in this story. After focusing dedicatedly on my job for a while, I returned to YMCA for volunteering. This meant that I would be required to do my day job with complete enthusiasm, and then squeeze in time during the rest of the day to volunteer at YMCA. I was hired to offer Career Support at YMCA's Employment Resource Centre. In addition to that, I was completely willing to explore other volunteering opportunities where I could use my experience & knowledge to guide others. I thought exactly what you are thinking of right now. How would I fit all the activity in a 24 hour day? However, I would somehow just manage. It didn't cause me any inconvenience or tiredness. In fact, I would look forward to the time when I would work and make some serious contribution to the society.

There's obviously a reason why I am mentioning this at this juncture of the story. Everything was flowing in order, right? I struggled, tried hard, volunteered, door knocked, and found myself a job. What would suddenly make me go back to volunteering? I am sure that's what you are thinking right now. We spoke about a few things that could help you in your journey, but how would going back to volunteering help you? It's not about volunteering, here. It is about being in absolute love with what you are doing. I loved helping people; you might love some other aspect of your job. It is your prerogative to do more at that. Add more experience to your role, learn a new skill, or simply do your job with added flair.

As immigrants, our first job might not exactly be what we desired. It might, at best, be a bread-and-butter job, one that gets you the money and helps you bring food to the table. If you perform that job simply to make you money, it will never work as your launch-pad to a glorified career. However, we don't get a chance to worry about that. We get a job, and we do it for the sake of it – without putting our heart and soul into it. Any job that you do can have something you like. You might care about it, because it is building experience on your resume. You might care about it, because it is helping you sponsor your new house. You might care about it, because it helps you bring some food on the table. This way, you will have a purpose to the job and that will significantly improve your performance. I remember having heard a story of a young student, who started working as 'Cashier' at a South Asian store. On the face of it, it was a survival job. However, he wanted to make a difference. He started printing inspirational messages and quotes on small sheets of paper that he would put into each shopping bag. Over a period of time, he started being recognized by the customers there and they would line up to be billed at his counter. A small quote in the shopping bag had made him indispensable at the store. There are so many other examples. You might have recently watched the video of a young U.S. student who raps his resume to employers. This way, he stands out. The video is viral now, and recruiters must be vying to hire him. Things that you do with your heart and soul can take you places.

Did that happen in my case? I was still working my first job and volunteering at YMCA. At this moment, I thought it was time for me to move on from my job. It was time for me to take up greater challenges, and make more significant contributions. Additionally, my contract was about to come to an end too. Hence, I had to start looking out again. I had been applying for positions in the Peel region and the response till now had been heartening. Those applications helped me get a temporary contract position at other non-profit organization in Peel region.

Alongside, I also picked up on my volunteer work for the time being. By now, I had already played various roles between volunteering and paid positions. I was performing all my roles really well, and that provided ample opportunity for employers to hire me. A case in point was another short term opportunity that came by, and I took that up right after my contract expired. This was an extremely different role from anything that I had done in the past. I was the Co-ordinator for an Employment Program. Once that contract was over, I hopped onto another challenging opportunity. I was required to meet with Canadian employers and talk to them about the virtues of hiring international candidates for a 6 to 8 week co-op placement. This role was one that I still remember, because it challenged me to the core. Moreover, it also got me introduced to many new people, a lot of who were employers.

In fact, my volunteering got me introduced to another facet of my personality. I was invited to speak at a few events, and share my story with immigrants. This was at multiple non-profit organizations, and I realized that this was another aspect of my work that I loved. I could instantly connect with multiple immigrants, and make an emphatic presentation on how they could move over their struggle period. I got this platform to be able to inspire them to move over the ordinary, and achieve something worthwhile in their lives. These talks got me to a larger stage. I was invited to MC a conference titled 'Immigrant's Civic Engagement: A Conference for Institutions and Organizations in Peel.' The conference played host to the who's who of the municipal, provincial, and federal governments. There were prominent faces in the audience, and I was to speak in front of all of them. Think of that as an opportunity. Not only did it boost my confidence as a speaker, I could network with some of the most influential people of Peel and Greater Toronto Area   Obviously, they gave me their feedback and also offered to stay in touch with me. I can proudly say that many of them are still connected with me.

From that day onwards, I have spoken at about 10 to 15 events each year. This could be for non-profit organizations, community colleges, award galas, conferences, focus groups, professional development institutions, etc. This was all because I loved what I was doing. Like the quote at the beginning of this story says; if you are not making someone's life better, you might just be wasting your time. I decided that I wanted to help the society, especially new immigrants. When you start your career in Canada, you should have a purpose too. It is that purpose that will make you go an inch ahead of everyone else, and that will reflect on what you ultimately achieve by the end of your career.

For all of you, I would strongly recommend that you continue to educate yourself to improve your prospects of growth. Volunteering also opens up a great platform for networking and adding valuable experience to your resume. One or both of these things, even when you are settled in your job, will gradually take you to newer heights. Please remember, though. When you do something, do it with passion; otherwise, you are wasting your time.

Dilnawaz Qamar (Mental Health Counselor, and one of Sukhjit's well-wishers) gives her take on the story:

"Everyone who is new to Canada knows that the period of transition after landing here is not easy. There are multiple concerns, worries and a number of adjustments to make. So was true for me. With very young children, I stayed at home and my husband started with a labor job. However, I didn't want to sit idle at home. Being mother of young children, I wanted to do something from home.

Few months after landing one of our family friends suggested me to go and see Sukhjit. He said he went to Sukhjit when he was new here. I went to visit him and my heart was full of doubts and my self-esteem very low. I didn't take my resume because I was sure that no matter how capable I was back home I won't be able to start my life from that level. I found in him a positive and encouraging man. After knowing my academic and work background he was very hopeful. I shared with him how I had been writing articles for a newspaper back home but I was not confident if I could ever write here in Canada. Sukhjit's response was very encouraging. He encouraged me to write. The thing that I liked most about him that his encouragement was not just a lip service. He helped me practically. Sukhjit shared some useful links and contact numbers with me and asked me to start writing. That was the first day that I felt that I will be able to work here.

It was through the confidence that Sukhjit gave me that my first article was printed soon after our first meeting. I felt an overwhelming joy when I was paid for the article without leaving the home. One year has passed and 5-6 articles had been printed. However, I didn't keep contact with Sukhjit for a while.

In 2016 when I felt that my elder daughter is young enough I planned to do a job. The first person that came across my mind was Sukhjit. I went to him and shared my concern with him. He welcomed me with a warm smile and listened to me actively. He shared few contact numbers and immediately sent me few job postings through email. Again it was through his contact and emails that I got a job in my field i.e. mental health counselor.

Sukhjit had been a positive influence in my 2 years of stay in Canada. The way he talks and impacts his clients in a positive way is enough to boost confidence of the clients that is a much needed skill to learn and grow in a professional setting. Without any doubt I owe my success in Canada to the sincere support and kindness of Sukhjit.

CHAPTER NINE

BECOMING A 'CHANGE' AGENT

"It will never rain more roses: when we want to have more roses, we must plant more roses" – George Eliot

ake a moment to yourself at this point, and ask yourself 'Has my life always been bright & upbeat?' Most of you would answer in the negative. There are times in your life when things simply refuse to fall in place. It is a feeling of absolute despair. As an immigrant, you are highly probable to experience this feeling- especially towards the beginning of your journey. You have moved to a new country, and everything seems to be completely alien. You aren't sure how to conduct yourself; most of us don't even know how to order a cup of coffee at Tim Horton's or any other cafe. I remember how in my initial days in Canada, I didn't understand what double-double and similar parlance would mean. I was used to walking up to the barista in India and say "Get me a cup of hot coffee / cold coffee, please." However, times don't take very long to change. With the passage of time, you will integrate into the society and also stitch a successful career for yourself. This understanding will always hold you in good stead.

If you remember from the last story, I was still in between jobs. My volunteering activity had picked up. At the same time, I was speaking at multiple events. All of this was keeping me busy and contended. In fact, an increasing number of renowned companies and not-for-profit organizations were seeking out my speaking or other voluntary skills. I knew getting a job wasn't very far either. Having the right position was imperative, though. This time, I wanted to get into a position that will help me pursue my passion of helping people. While performing my role as a volunteer and while speaking at various events, I had the pleasure of meeting a range of different people. These were people from diverse walks of life, and going through varying struggles. Think of the life of a refugee. These were people who had escaped home to find a safer haven, one they found in Canada. Their previous experiences with torture, violence, and injustice were still lingering in their minds. This was compounded by all the other problems that a new Canadian can be faced with: Understanding the public transit system, finding the right house, getting a job, immigration-related paperwork, and more. Then there were students, who had their set of challenges. And obviously, I would also meet new immigrants into the country.

I used to have mixed feelings at the end of the day. There was a feeling of melancholy for what all of these people were experiencing. That used to be combined with the feeling of triumph, though. Triumph for being able to have helped these people in some way. It was this positive energy that helped me have a newfound desire to help people. My only tools were volunteering and my speeches (and hopefully my future job!), and it was imperative that I made my work more purposeful. Everything I did had to address these people's most pressing issues. After much contemplation, I thought to myself that the best approach to take was of 'Motivation' and 'Positivity.'

Here was a new dimension to my work. Every time, I would be speaking in front of an audience; I would make sure that I motivated them. I had to give them instances of my life about how persistence and hard-work could bring me the desired rewards. However, that wouldn't have happened without 'Belief.' People who believe that their work will reap them great results are more likely to succeed in their endeavor. My story is a prime example of the same. I continued to do all the good work with complete belief, and everything else seemed to have simply fallen in place for me. That's why our point of discussion, during my speeches, had to shift from how difficult Canada was for newcomers to how these new members of the Canadian society can make a difference.

As they say, "The biggest room in the world is the room for improvement." With every speech and each interaction with immigrants, refugees, students, and all others; I would learn something and try to improve. And then, I love the following words from Nelson Mandela too "Education is the most powerful weapon we can use to change the world." Thus, I started reading all the more. I didn't want to just talk about my experiences, but also share what some of the other successful immigrants had to say about making it large in Canada. In the process, I came across a few people who had a strong influence on my thought process. In fact, they even made me realize the significance of the work that I was performing. They helped me understand that I was not just a speaker, but a 'Change Agent.' Among them were two people, who need a special mention here. They gave me the energy-boost in order to continue to do the good work. I was trying to explain both instances here, but I would rather share what they wrote to/for me:

INSTANCE # 01

"My meeting with Sukhjit Singh was an unforgettable event. It had been a few months in Canada as a landed immigrant. Upon landing here, I was experiencing cultural shock. In a new life, a new start, with two little girls. I was advised by a friend to visit North York Library for a talk with immigrants. I saw a man in a yellow turban, who introduced himself and then told us his story and his experiences in Canada as an immigrant. I felt as though he was talking about my experiences and feelings. I could relate with it all. I feel Sukhjit Singh is a selfless person who made a difference and is helping new immigrants, regardless of their religion or creed, and till day he guides me. I take him as an angel who came in my life only to help and guide me."

I was always thinking that trying to help immigrants in every way was a core part of my life. This woman, though, made me realize that I was heralding real change in people's lives. This wasn't a matter of taking pride in, but something that placed more responsibilities on my shoulders. More importantly, this was another example of how positivity changes lives. Compare this letter with the hate email I had received earlier. I could have easily given up on Canada after that letter, but I instead used that as a stepping stone for a glorious future.

INSTANCE # 02

"Do you believe in alchemy!!

Some days are better than others but there are some that get engraved on the templates of the mind and can rightly be called as experiences that serve as a stimulus for continuous improvement and growth. My visit to Royal Ontario Museum for the Passages Canada event with **Mr. Sukhjit Singh** was one of such days.

I came to Canada with lot of dreams and aspirations but the first things I heard were "It's a difficult country for immigrants!! Getting a job is not that easy!! Build a network to get a job!!" and I took it as a reality and there started a downward spiral of negativity and in the days to come I started feeling that I may never make it here. I flunked interviews after interview. I started trying to understand the Canadian culture in all its aspects, ironically to get a job! I was trying to meet as many people as possible, to impress them, again only to get a job! A mere job had become the principle focus of my life. Those were the days that reflected the psyche of almost every new immigrant who is not as lucky as me to meet someone like Mr. Sukhjit Singh.

Within 8 months of my arrival, I was sure that I will not get a job in Canada. Those days made me realize that mere breathing lungs and a pumping heart are the most misleading signs of "being alive". One has to have something to look forward to- that's called "being alive". I didn't had any such goal, purpose, aspiration or ambition when I met **Mr. Sukhjit Singh** at Mississauga Library for the first time, again with a purpose to procure a survival job at some retail store or fast food joint to earn some money in my summer break. I talked to him for just about half an hour that day. In this small conversation he acted mainly as a listener, but I still don't know why by the end of our meeting I had made up my mind that I will not do anything that doesn't serve my mission or purpose of life. I knew that I have just met someone whose ½ an hour of positivity is way more than all the negativity I have accumulated in these 8 months. I decided to interact with him more frequently.

Spending another day with Mr Sukhjit Singh, this time at Royal Ontario Museum, gave me the opportunity to observe him more closely and realize something very abstract yet important. I observed that Mr Singh interacts with others (read "his own self") beyond the restrictions of culture and language and embraces everyone with an open attitude, warm gestures and a genuine smile. He creates a jamboree of happiness around. This reinforces the teaching of Bhagwad Gita (Hindu Scripture) which emphasizes the oneness of human race. On that day, it felt as if I already know everyone in Canada.

During his speech he showed the audience a receipt of his porter services, a Canadian flag gifted to him, a magazine in which he advertised himself to get a job when he landed here and other such details of his life and journey!! I still wonder whether he knew that he will share his story someday as a speaker I think so, as if that would not have been so, he would not have been an epitome of positivity who can turn around the thought of many, and hence create success, that is "life well lived" for many like me.

*To conclude, I will again take this opportunity to thank **Mr. Singh** for being an alchemist in every sense of the word. Although I don't believe in superstitions but strongly believe that something changed in me after meeting this wonderful person. I cracked my first interview (after meeting him) as a physician and got a job appropriate to my experience and education or else I would have been doing a job that doesn't synchronize with my mission and purpose in life.*

Now do you believe in alchemy!!"

Wasn't this exceptionally sweet on part of someone to write so well about a speaker? I was happy at the fact that he used the word 'Positivity' frequently in his write-up. That's what I like to do. I am not a recruitment agency, and I can't connect people with jobs. Similarly, I can't help them find a house, connect with friends, or achieve all other basic amenities. I can be a 'Change Agent,' though; one who emphasizes on positivity and persistence. I want to guide them on the things they need to do to settle into the Canadian society. More importantly, I want to harp on how all of that would be a waste if the person would be loaded with negativity. Finding toxic people isn't difficult for a new immigrant, but dodging them on the way is what I want to teach them.

In fact, all my effort of speaking about positive energy and motivation rubbed off on me too. I was invited back to my first company for another contract assignment, this time in the position that I was aspiring for. So, now I had a job too that will keep me challenged and financially content. Moreover, I decided to simultaneously take up more challenging volunteering roles, and even undertook the mission of promoting volunteerism in the Peel region. To my surprise, the media was quick to pick up on this and I was made the unofficial ambassador of volunteering in Peel. I was invited on T.V. shows to speak about my passion for being a change agent, and I also got the pleasure of speaking at Ministry of Citizenship, Ontario's Volunteer Appreciation Event. Who would have known that a few years later (for 2012), I would go on to win the 'Newcomer Gem Volunteer' award by Volunteer MBC. This was my first award in Canada, and it meant a lot to me. Doing all the great work is superb, but being appreciated for it every now and them lends on the added to energy to continue. I shall continue to strive in order to herald a positive change in your lives.

'

CHAPTER TEN

TRANSFERABLE SKILLS

"It is possible to fly without motors, but not without knowledge and skill" —Wilbur Wright

*L*et us assume that you were in an interview right now, and someone asked you "What are the things that you do well?" What would your answer be? Think about it. There's some empty space on this page to let you write down (if you want) all those things that you do exceptionally well. These are those things that will get you hired for your preferred position:

_____

_____

_____

_____

What did you come up with? In most of my previous experiences, I have had people who haven't answered the questions correctly. People would say "I am a wonderful teacher." Someone else would say "I am great with I.T." These answers aren't incorrect, but my journey in Canada has taught me to rely on those skills, instead, that are readily transferable to other job positions.

Behind what we do really well is a set of skills that helps us perform the role better. It's that set of skills that needs to be identified to succeed in your career. This is because most of the skills that you possess can be transferred to a completely different role. Having this knowledge can go a long way in broadening the kind of job roles that you think you are interested in.

I started off my career in Oman as a Computer Instructor & Technician. That related well with my educational qualification, and I used to enjoy the role to its core. During my association with the organization, I went on to take more important roles. In addition to what I was doing, I became a member of the Academic Council. Following are some of the other tasks I took up along the way:

- Lecturer

- Member of Information Technology Committee

- Part of the Student Performance Mentoring System

- Chief Fire Warden: in-charge of the campus, which at any given time was filled with over 500 students and staff members

- Planned & Executed a popular workshop, named 'Student Management Skills.'

- Designed & Delivered short-term courses, based on industry needs.

I was also a Visiting Faculty at IGNOU (Oman Branch), where I used to teach management and MIS related courses to students, pursuing their Masters. Looking at all of this, what do you think I would strive to achieve when I moved to Canada? As many of you might have guessed, I tried to secure a teaching position here. I knocked on numerous doors and applied for various jobs, but I couldn't break into the industry. It was perhaps because I didn't possess any Canadian credentials at that time to support my profile. That was when I decided to broaden my horizon, and look for anything that would help me pay my bills. Obviously, I soon started thinking that all my teaching skills and I.T. skills were in vain. I would now be doing something that hardly relates to my core skills. I cursed myself for having moved here. Have you gone through that feeling too? Most immigrants have. They suddenly start feeling that they need to change their industry and lose all that they had learned in their previous experience.

With time, though, I realized that real skills are those that are transferable. It is not the industry that matters. In fact, it is those transferable skills that will determine your performance at a job and your satisfaction with it. Let's take the example of teaching. In my initial days in Canada, I used to be extremely dissatisfied with not having got a teaching position. However, my real skill wasn't teaching. My real skills were public speaking, communication, and being able to explain my point well. I transferred all of those skills to the speeches that I made. If you remember from the earlier stories, my volunteering got me invited to a few events as a Key-note speaker. It didn't take me very long to transfer all my skills and perform well. In fact, my speeches also helped me be introduced to several other important people.

Even in my first job, where I was required to counsel new immigrants to Canada, I could use most of my teaching skills. I was required to be a good communicator in order to pass on the right message. At the same time, I needed to be patient with my audience and take them through the process of settlement in a new country - step-by-step.

Most of us – new immigrants to Canada – make the same mistake that I committed at the beginning of my journey in this country. I kept trying to find a job in my industry, and completely closed my eyes to all other opportunities where I could effectively use my skills. That, in fact, reflects in our resume too. We focus on our job responsibilities in our previous employments, instead of emphasizing on the skills we used and the kind of results we generated. One of my close friends is great at making presentations. He used to be a visiting faculty at educational institutes in India. Moreover, he is a very good writer too. In his early days here, he kept trying to either have a teaching or a writing position. However, he finally decided to get into sales and he was successful with that. He effectively used his writing skills to create compelling email marketing campaigns and customer proposals. At the same time, his presentation skills helped him convince his customers better than his competition.

I would like to encourage you all to go back to the first page of this story and note down that set of skills that you possess. You can then distinguish skills on the basis of your proficiency. The ones that you are good at can be honed. Other skills that you have basic knowledge of can be worked upon through certification courses, volunteering, or other such means. This will also solidify your skill set and strengthen your profile for future opportunities. Once you have these skills ready, you need to take your resume and make it skill-based rather than being job-based. Focus on the skills you used rather than the tasks you performed.

Coming back to my story; you might remember from earlier in this story that I was part of numerous committees in Oman. I always thought that this was just a role I performed as a professor. However, it had more to it. I could only understand the value of that skill when a few of my mentors in Canada advised me to back up my experience with Canadian education. I completed a quick online course on 'How Boards Works?' What did that lead to? That move got me an offer to co-chair a committee at a non-profit group. I suddenly realized that I had the skill to be able to contribute to committees, and I enjoyed the role thoroughly as well. Going forward, I used this experience to be on the board of various other organizations. It wasn't exactly in an academic set-up, but I was using my skills the best way. I served on the board of Peel Newcomer Strategy Group, Peel District School Board , Ontario, Ministry of Labor, , VolunteerMBC, Heritage Minutes – Passages Canada, and many others. In fact, this experience helped me get hired as a consultant with two big brands in Canada. We shall talk about that in the next few chapters. For now, though, let us all remember that it is possible to fly without motors, but not without knowledge and skill. We are all gifted with some skills that help us perform a task better than others. Let us identify those skills and brace ourselves for our flight to glory.

CHAPTER ELEVEN
HOMECOMING

"Having a place to go – is a home. Having someone to love – is a family. Having both is a blessing."—Donna Hedges

"*C*an *you hear me?" – I asked my wife.*

"Everyone can." She said "Why are you speaking so loudly?"

For some reason, airplanes tend to get the better of me. My hearing abilities get impaired and I start talking very loudly. This flight wasn't any different. It had been more than a few hours since take-off, but my ears were still kind-of blocked. I would keep trying to clean my ears, but that will obviously not help. I couldn't wait to get off that plane. However, it wasn't just the discomfort that made me want to get off. I was, instead, extremely excited about setting foot upon my homeland after two long years. That excitement will literally push me off my chair – all geared up to deplane at the first opportunity. Yes! I was going to India. I was headed towards that place where my parents were........that place that had populated my thoughts for much of the last 2 years.

I started planning for this vacation from a few months earlier. If you remember, I had secured another contract position at my first company. I absolutely loved this job, and it was giving me the opportunity to learn, grow, and contribute. Alongside, I was doing a whole host of other things. For starters, I got to work at other not for profit organization as a casual staff member. Alongside, I was also pursuing a professional development certificate course. This was towards becoming a certified career and employment information specialist. That was a good learning experience, and that helped me improve my performance at the job. My current position at the company was to help newcomers get into the job market. Hence, my certification in career and employment information worked seamlessly with that.

As I mentioned earlier, though, mine was a contract position and it was to end in October of 2011. Thus, I started planning with my family about a trip to India right after the end of the contract. After 2 years of continuous struggle and hard-work, all of us in the family needed some time off from work. We booked our tickets and planned to be in India for the whole month of December. As long as this trip might sound to you, we still felt short of time. That's what happens when you go home. No trip is long enough.

Coming back to that flight...We were now about 3 hours away from landing in Delhi, and our hearts were already pounding. Our enthusiasm knew no bounds, and it wasn't just my daughter. We were all behaving like kids, trying to imagine what India would be like. Would it have changed in those 2 years or would it be the same welcoming place that we remember it as? How will our parents react, meeting us after a couple of years? I remember how my mother always told me that 'Every minute without her kids feels like ages for a mother.' I was wondering what 2 years would have done to her. Would she have aged in this period? How about my father? I used to be his best friend and most trusted companion. What would life have been for him in those 2 years?

Most immigrants who go back to their home country for the first time might feel the same way. It is that difficult-to-express feeling that combines many different emotions together. You smile from ear to ear, but your eyes are wet. It is an oxymoron that can't be put in words. I remember how my wife & I would look at the flight path to see how far we were from our destination. As soon as our plane entered the Indian airspace, our enthusiasm knew no bounds. We were now in striking distance of our destination. All that we had been imagining for the last few months would unfold in just a couple of hours.

There's another irony in this story. You are unbelievably excited for the months leading up to your trip to India. However, that drains you out emotionally. By the time your flight lands in India, you are so tired that you tend to become unexpressive. Perhaps, that's also because you are in a state of trance to be back in your country. Only those who have lived away from home for years can understand what I am trying to express here.

Anyway, our flight landed in India and our parents were enthusiastically waiting for us at the airport. Punjabi's know how to party, and they are not bound by the place. As soon as we got out of the airport premises, the party commenced right then. Many of our relatives had made it to the airport to welcome us and that happened in perfect Punjabi style. There were happy people, there were drums, and there was zeal. That's all you need to get the party rolling.

Wait….that is how all my friends in Canada thought my arrival in India would pan out. That's what most of the immigrants get, when they return to their home town. You have people, drums, and a lot of festivities. My family's different. My parents believe that they don't want to be overly excited about my arrival, because it will hurt more when I go back. They wanted to go about their life as usual. Right or wrong; that's the approach they followed. So, there were no drums and no party at the airport. All I had was my father, who had come to receive me. My mother was waiting at home. I am sure she couldn't wait, but she didn't let that excitement spill out.

For the first few days of my trip, we just unwound and spent time with family. At the same time, I strived to pursue my passion too. When I was planning this trip in Canada, I was wondering how I could help Canadian newcomers during my vacation. While there was no way of doing that, I thought I could try to prepare those individuals who were on the verge of flying to Canada. I am talking about new PR holders who haven't yet left for Canada.

The Government of Canada runs an orientation program for new residents. This is a 2 day workshop that acquaints new residents with Canada – its weather, house market, job situation, etc. I had participated in that program before moving to Canada, and I had thought that the program was a wonderful opportunity for new residents. It got them prepared for the things to come. I was such a big fan of the program and participated in it so religiously that there was a video made on me a little while later. We shall talk about that in the next few stories. For now, let's focus on this story. So, I thought that being a speaker in that orientation workshop will let me share my experience with new residents. I wanted them to see the journey from the eyes of an immigrant. I quickly scouted my contacts in India and Ottawa to see if someone could get me introduced with the organizers of that workshop. My volunteering and talks had bestowed me with some very helpful contacts. One of those got me connected someone at the organization that executes those workshops around the world. I got lucky, and I was offered the opportunity to speak at one of those workshops in the beautiful city of Chandigarh, Punjab (India). This opportunity added more value to my trip. Not only did I enjoy with my family & friends, but I also got a chance to pursue my passion. While speaking with new immigrants, I managed to relate with them and tell them stories of what to expect. I could tell them how a simple task like boarding the bus can be a challenge in a new country, and what's the best way of tackling that. It went off very well. This balance of home and work was just the perfect dose of energy I needed to get back to Canada and continue my journey. I told you earlier that a trip to home is always short. That's what we felt too. We extended our 1 month trip to 3 long months to return in February.

There are times when we just focus on work. I had read somewhere of how work was like a rubber ball. If you dropped it for a while, it will bounce back to you. However, family is like a glass ball. You drop it, and there are chances that it will be shattered. Hence, it is important for us to take that break that we deserve. Our family deserves to have a share of our time as it is the catalyst of our growth. Without the support of our family, we might not have the strength to fight the world. Equally important is to remember the importance of home. Home is where dreams are seen and achieved. Home is that shelter where we feel safe. Go back sometime, if you can, because there's no other place on earth that will make you feel as calm.

My vacation to home worked very well for me. On my return, I got a short-term contract position with a community college in Mississauga, Ontario (Canada). Working as an academic recruiter, I was required to recruit students for a program. The program was designed for internationally trained and educated professionals and help them work on their soft skills and job hunting techniques. As soon as I was about to complete my contract there, I was excited about another short term contract position- this time as a member of the provincial parliament. I was thrilled about the prospects of closely learning about the political system of Canada. As imagined, it was a great learning experience for me.

During this period, I continued to volunteer. From the beginning till now, I had the fortune of volunteering for the following reputed organizations:

- YMCA as

  o Facilitator

  o YMCA-ERC as Resume Expert

  o Mentor at eNIC - Pre-Arrival Program for Canadian Immigrants

- Indus Community Services (Formally known as India Rainbow Community Services of Peel) as Project Assistant

- Peel Newcomer Strategy Group as a Co-Chair: Social, Civic inclusion of Newcomer to Canada.

- Peel District School Board as

- o Member: Parents Involvement committee (representing Mississauga)

- Region of Peel

  - o Family Literacy program facilitator

  - o www.immigrationpeel.ca web portal video

- Ontario Ministry of Labour

  - o Co-chair: Small Business Task group

- Canadian Immigrant Integration Program (CIIP) – Ambassador

- Passages Canada

  - o Member, Speaker Bureau

  - o Heritage Minutes Advisory Committee

- Volunteer MBC

  - o Volunteer Ambassador

  - o Board of Directors

CHAPTER TWELVE
CONNECTING THE DOTS

"The currency of real networking is not greed but generosity" —
Keith Ferrazzi

All throughout this book, we have spoken about various concepts that don't feature very high in an immigrant's priority list. Volunteering is a strong case in point. I am a huge fan of volunteering, and that would have reflected in the way I have presented that concept in this book thus far. However, it is not all just about doing un-paid work. That is what we think of volunteering, don't we? We, as immigrants, think of it as doing free work, and that of course isn't something we do until we are settled ourselves. However, volunteering is about a cycle. It connects you with people, you engage with them, and it promptly increases the size of that group of people who could either hire you or recommend you for the position of your choice. As the quote at the beginning of this story tells you, the currency of real networking is generosity. That subtly tells you that you can't start volunteering with the thought of getting a job. Every step in the way is a milestone in itself. Your job is to focus on those milestones, and ensure that you focus enough on them. As you continue to do some good work, you get to exhibit your skills to more people. These are people who are influenced by you and will certainly come back in your life someday with a piece of news that sweeps you off your feet.

So, coming back to my story. I had returned from my long trip to India. Coming back home was a mixed feeling. I was obviously extremely dejected. India and Canada are two different worlds, and present different scenarios. When you spend time in the frenzied streets of India, you get used to the continuous enthusiasm and activity. You are never alone there. The sheer number of people around you, whether you know them or not, never lets you be lonely. On the other hand, Canada is quiet. Once you reach the street where you live, you will hardly see any people. So, you get your privacy but you miss that rush of zeal and gusto that flows through the hearts and lives of Indians in India. You miss those street vendors around your home. You can walk down anytime of the day, and treat yourself to some lip-smacking food. You miss your domestic help; the boy who wipes the floor at your house, that young guy who washes your car every day, the middle-aged man who comes to buy your newspapers and other recyclables, and all those other people. While this was in the back of my mind, my bonding with Canada had strengthened during my time away. I started this paragraph by saying 'Coming back home was a mixed feeling.' When I read that sentence again, I was pleasantly surprised that Canada was now my home. After all the struggles that an immigrant goes through, it takes a while for you to love the country enough to call it home. You will care for the country, but your home will always be what's left behind. Your mind will be populated by thoughts of your parents and all your loving relatives, those who miss you sorely and would wish for you to return someday. However, the beauty of Canada and its people is that they accept you as theirs almost instantly. It is that feeling of belonging that makes you feel at home, sooner rather than later. My feeling of belonging was now arriving.

I did not have a lot of time to analyze my state of mind, though. My contract at my previous company had ended before I left for India. Hence, I had to swing into action immediately and re-initiate my job search. The good part of it this time was that I didn't have to start from scratch. There were contacts I had established already, and I needed to connect back with them. At the same time, I was back into the field of volunteering and that was helping me engage with new people every day. All of this combined together to ensure that I had a job in no time. I mentioned to you in the previous chapter that I got a short term contract position with a popular and well established community college in Mississauga. While the position was just 3 months, it was to help me learn a lot. I was playing the role of an 'Academic Recruitment Specialist' at this college, and it was to introduce me to the various facets of academia in Canada. The role required me to connect with internationally educated and skilled immigrants to get them enrolled in our skill-development programs. Most of these immigrants, like me, came to Canada with immense skill and education. However, translating that into a recognized job in Canada was hard. This course was supposed to help these new Canadians put their career in top gear. It will not just help them convert their qualification into Canadian equivalent, but also connect them with more people.

By the virtue of the fact that I was in community engagement since a long time, this was not going to be hard for me. Through my volunteering work, I had been engaging with new immigrants and consulting them on how to advance their lives and careers in Canada. I extended the same, now on behalf of this community college. One of my close friends always says that you should only talk about a product or service that you are completely convinced about. I was convinced about this program. That used to reflect in the way that I spoke with immigrants. This skill helped ensure that I performed well. Again, this is a learning I use in my life. Regardless of the terms of my engagement with a person or an organization, I always try to give my very best. I will only take up something when I know that I can do it with my heart and soul. That includes my volunteer work as well. Many people tend to make the mistake of taking voluntary work lightly. If you aren't being paid for something doesn't mean that you don't need to meet your commitment. If you promise to do something, you need to make sure that you do it right. My good work with the community college ensured that I had a point of contact and a reference for life.

During this engagement with the college, I was also doing a lot of exciting volunteer work on the side. I was trying to introduce a new way to reach out to the community and engage various stakeholders. By my experience, I always leaned towards new Canadians who needed a network and some help. I was so passionate about helping my fellow immigrants that I was thinking about it every second of the day. At that point of my life, I had another milestone. Immigration Peel featured me in a video of theirs. The video presented information on how someone could navigate through the immigrationpeel. ca website. More than being an accomplishment, it was a testimony of the work that I had put in towards making Canada more immigrant-friendly. I still very fondly look back at that video and feel proud of having done what I did in those early days.

A new element of my work that had been lately picking up as well was speaking at events. I had started doing that before my trip to India, and I continued with that after my return as well. What I liked about these talks was that they served two purposes. First, I could speak with new immigrants about my journey and how I adapted to various changes in life. Second, I could also vent. There are times when you want to share your story with people. You want to vent, and those talks could serve the purpose for me. After speaking with the participants of those events, I would realize that I was perhaps among the luckier lot of people. There are some new Canadians who face an incredible amount of hardship. I used to come across heart-wrenching stories of people who had toiled without success in their early days in this country. If you are someday experiencing that feeling of dejection and helplessness, talk to any other immigrant you know You will come across stories that will make you thank god for what you have.

My talks, at different venues and for varying audiences, also got me very far in terms of my contacts. I was connecting the dots as I was meeting with key people in the fraternity. The events I conducted and attended during my stint with the community college helped too. One such person I met because of my events and socializing was a lady who is very close to my heart till date. She has always been extremely helpful to me and has tried her best to help me settle into the Canadian scheme of things. She was, then, a key member of Ontario's Parliamentarian office. I met with her during a public event, and she was impressed by what I shared. She was impressed (at least that is what I would like to think) and agreed to stay in touch with me. However, agreeing to share her contact information was one thing; actually getting in touch with me was completely another. She did contact me, and asked me about my contract with the college. I was surprised that she still remembered that my contract with the college was coming to an end soon. She asked me to share my resume with her so that she can see if there was something she could do for me. Can you believe what happened next? This compassionate and extremely helpful woman got me an interview call from the MPP's office. Can you imagine how I would have felt that day? I had been working through various facets of community service, and now I had the opportunity of working with the MPP. Till a few days back, I wasn't even prepared to call Canada home. Now, I was going to be serving this country way more extensively than I had ever thought. Of course, I just had an interview call for now, but the prospects of working there was making me excited already. I am always extremely well prepared for my interviews. In this case, I spent additional time in conversing myself with a lot of information about the MPP. I read extensively about the role that an MPP plays, and the things that I could do there. With my experience and skill, there was a lot that I could change. All this hard work paid off and I was hired for a contract position there. I was covering one of their employee's maternity leave for a year. However, this was enough for me. I knew that I could use this opportunity to learn, grow, and impress. Like some of my previous contracts, I was prepared to work hard and grow in stature.

By God's grace, I have been extremely lucky through my entire journey in Canada. My job with the MPP's Office is a prime example of the same. I finished my contract with the college on Friday and started at the MPP office on Monday. I didn't have to spend a single day in actively searching for a job. However, I also credit this achievement to my dedication, passion, and large network.

In the beginning of the chapter, I spoke about networking being about giving more than taking back. When I speak in front of my audiences, I do it with a genuine interest in helping them. I want to give them something to take home and think about. However, with the passage of time; I have realized that this has helped me connect the dots and build a strong network. It's like a game you play where every dot you connect takes you further towards your vision. My volunteering got me my first paid position and my passionate way of talking at events touched the heart of the lady who got me referred to the MPP Office.

So, give up your inhibitions and engage. Engage with your community; engage with the people you like and who matter. However, always do it with the intention to help. Perhaps, you can help young kids learn a new language or work at a company to set up their IT system or just consult someone. It is like good karma; it always comes back to you.

CHAPTER THIRTEEN

FLYING HIGH

"Next to excellence is the appreciation of it." —William Makepeace Thackeray

ood job' – these two words are so dear to all of us. We spend hours and days and months and years to get someone to say that to us. It is that feeling of having achieved an objective; of having been recognized for the kind of work that we have done. I wouldn't blame you if you thought that this was so rudimentary. You would think that all you need to do is to work in silence and let your success make all the noise. That's what I thought for a long time in my career. However, my move to Canada made me realize that I wasn't right. I could be casual about the significance of appreciation because I would get it regularly. I would work away in silence and something that I did would create a buzz. That kept me going. That small pat on the back would ignite the spark. When I moved to Canada, though, those small pats on the back were few and far apart. For a long period of time during my initial phase in this country, I was working away to find myself a decent job. In this brief period, all I received was desperation and despair. Every passing day would make me more stressed about my future here. However, things did turn around and appreciations at different levels satiated my need to be recognized for my performance. None of those appreciations, though, were as powerful as the one I received in the year 2012.

So, I was in the 3rd year of my journey in Canada. I had returned from India, and the following period was full of excitement and energy. A contract job at a community college helped me build more contacts and learn more. Upon the completion of that contract, I had moved on to a position at the MPP Office. I was absolutely thrilled to have an opportunity of working closely with the MPP. Being there was going to acquaint me with the Canadian scheme of things. I was to get to engage with the community more deeply.

During the initial phase of my engagement with the MPP Office, I was fortunate to have some really helpful colleagues by my side. These colleagues (and now friends) were compassionate about the challenges I could face, because of my newness to the industry. Moreover, being just 3 years old in Canada; I was still not conversant with some of the systems; especially the ones that concerned Ontario's parliamentarian. However, my colleagues made sure that none of this posed any threat to my performance at work. They would spend time with me each day in training me on the system and the tasks that I was required to perform. In response to that, I was trying my best to learn the ropes of the position as fast as possible. I had previous experience of case management, and that went a long way in making my life easy at the office. Moreover, I used to always do extra reading at home in order to be completely prepared at work.

Being in my position there was also introducing me to things that I wasn't aware of earlier. I had never imagined that an MPP Office could be as busy. Obviously, we all know the amount of work that is put in by these offices at the time of the election. You need to reach out to the community and communicate your points in a clear and concise manner. Contrary popular opinion, though, the amount of work that an MPP needs to do seemed to have risen after the election period. I was previously under the impression that an MPP was only supposed to visit dining events and make other appearances. This was certainly a large part of what an MPP needed to do to stay connected with the people of the community. However, this wasn't all the tasks that needed to be performed at that office. By watching an MPP work from close quarters, I realized that they were way more extensively involved with the community than just making appearances at dining events. The MPP Office was engrossed in some real social work. There used to be tons of mails, phone calls, and emails received by the office and we always tried our best to respond to those at the earliest. These communications used to be complaints or requests that community members had. The challenge was to find an agreeable solution for them. Being an MPP Office, we could not simply change rules or amend policies. However, we could put our people's points forward. The MPP could represent the people of the community at Queen's Park in Toronto.

In addition to addressing and redressing all the issues and problems that people had, the MPP also spent time in social work. The team used to pick up causes in the community that needed support, and then it will do what it could to make a difference. During my stint here, I got to visit certain events with the MPP and also had the opportunity to directly converse with the community members, including citizens, immigrants, students, and refugees. My compassion while dealing with people and their issues got me recognized within the team. I was appreciated for being honest, humble, and helpful. These are the 3 H's of my life that I am extremely proud of.

This position was also aligning very well with all my volunteering activity. The eventual goal of my life had turned into helping my community in the best manner possible. All of us have passions. Someone is passionate about a sport, while some other person loves writing. If we get to turn our passion into our profession, every day at the job becomes fun. That is what happened with me. I had quickly realized that I wanted to use my existing skills to help immigrants and other people of the region. All my positions were geared towards that. In fact, there were times when I spent more time on volunteering than on my paid work.

If all of this wasn't giving me the high already, there was something else that was going to change my life. All throughout this book, I kept telling you how I was striving hard to bring myself and my family to the same position (socially and professionally) that I governed in Oman and India. I wanted to enjoy the same level of respect and appreciation here. All of these jobs that I performed were contributing towards bringing me close to my dream. However, what was really giving my career a thrust forward was volunteering. I know I talk about volunteering way too much, but it has done enough to my career to be able to command that level of recall in my story.

It had now been 3 years since I had made 'THE' move of life, leaving behind a comfortable life for a new adventure. In these 3 years, I had engaged with multiple not-for-profit organizations. Most, if not all, of these organizations were still in touch with me. I used to talk at multiple events or perform any other task that I thought could be of help to them. At this phase of life, I had taken a step further in the cycle. I realized very quickly that all I had got was 24 hours. I, in my personal capability, could only do so much. It was time that I tried to expand the horizon. That is when I came up with the idea of promoting volunteering in the Peel region. If you remember, I did make a cursory mention about this earlier. As an unofficial ambassador of volunteering in the Peel area and later became the official Volunteer ambassador at Volunteer MBC, I was talking to various people at different places about the virtues of volunteering. I was convincing them about how giving to the society always ensures that you get back something that's valuable to you. Not only are we talking about the satisfaction of being able to use your skills in order to help the society, it is also about building contacts and generating opportunities for the future. Such was the scale of this initiative that people were starting to take notice. More people were asking about volunteering to me, and others were spreading the word. I was invited by television channels to do shows with them, and tell them about why a newcomer was focusing on volunteering instead of talking about how to find a job. They wanted to know about my story, and broadcast that to the world. On similar lines, I also received an invitation to speak at 2 key events by the Ontario Ministry of Citizenship and Immigration. One of those events was their annual volunteer appreciation gala.

Among all this publicity, word of mouth, TV coverage, and high-profile events; some key people in the community took immediate interest. These people and organizations saw real value in what I was doing, and wanted me to have the motivation to continue doing that. That was when came along my very first award in Canada. Volunteer MBC presented me with the 'Newcomer Gem Volunteer Award' in the year 2013. As you would have guessed already, this award was a game changer in my life. Working hard, coming up with ideas, receiving appreciation at work, connecting with new people, and everything else was wonderful. However, receiving an award of this stature made me believe even more in my potential. I was flying high, and who knew that we were just getting started?

Adriane Beaudry (Past Manager, Volunteer Engagement & Programming at Volunteer MBC) gives her take on the story:

"I still remember the day Sukhjit walked into my office. His infections smile spread across his face as he talked about the importance of volunteering and how he's been telling everyone, especially newcomers, how important volunteering is... that it's a great way to get to know your new community, meet new people, enjoy new positive experiences and have a great time doing it. He let me know that he was already a huge supporter of Volunteer MBC as an organization helping connect people who want to volunteer, with organizations that need them and that is why he wanted to formally join our team of volunteers. From that day forward, Sukhjit has been one of our strongest supporters! Wherever he goes, he brings our literature, spreads the word of volunteering and even sat on our Board of Directors to help strengthen volunteer engagement in the community."

CHAPTER FOURTEEN

BECOMING ONE OF TOP 25 CANADIAN IMMIGRANTS

"Sweat it out. You never know when that sweat releases a beautiful rainbow." – Sukhjit Singh

*L*et's assume that you had to get to the top of a tall building. Would you try to jump your way to the top? If you aimed to leap to the top, you will most certainly experience a big fall. Except for those movies in the 1990's, where the protagonist was nothing shy of a super-hero, I can't think of any other example of someone reaching the top without planning a plausible route.

Answering my own question, I will first enter the building premises. You can consider various entrances into the premises, and pick the one that's best suited to your current location. Once you are inside the premises, you find the closest elevator. You would have most certainly been to buildings where the elevator takes forever to arrive at your floor. There have been occasions where I have saved time by climbing the stairs for a few floors until I get the elevator. You can keep waiting at the ground level, and in fact waste more time than taking the stairs. Taking the stairs also ensures that your knees, thigh muscles, and heart are trained and prepared to take some extra pressure if the elevator malfunctions on the way.

I spent three quarters of a page in my book talking about how to get to the top of a tall building. It is because this trip to the top of a building very closely represents an individual's journey to new heights and unprecedented accomplishments. If we try to quickly get to where we want to, most times we end up nowhere. Also, success stories that are extremely simple are generally short-lived. You will have those moments when you don't see light at the end of the tunnel. However, such moments keep you prepared for what needs to be done. It is like training your knees, thigh muscles, and heart for times when the elevator malfunctioned. Your eyes will learn the art of patience and exploration. If you stay calm and keep exploring, your eyes will definitely meet that bright glimmer of hope that will illuminate your path to glory. When I speak to my audiences, I strongly advise them to stay patient. Small steps can lead to great leaps.

When I look back at my journey thus far in Canada, it looks tantalizingly close to a jigsaw puzzle. Every piece of the puzzle came together one-by-one to eventually create the beautiful picture. It all started with my willingness to go out cold calling. I dropped my resume at numerous places, and that created umpteen connections for me in a new country. From there I moved on to volunteering, and that held me in very good stead too. Not only did I build new connections, I also generated some job / consultancy opportunities for myself. Hard work at each of those job opportunities finally got me in proximity with my goals. It got me to where I wanted to at that phase of my life.

In the year 2013, I was the recipient of the 'Newcomer Gem Volunteer Award.' That transformed me. I have heard people say that it's all in the mind. However, I only realized that when I won the award. I was being recognized for my work within the sector. Plus, I got in the limelight and people wanted to know my story. All of this was wonderful. However, it was that sense of accomplishment that stirred up my self-esteem. All this while, as an immigrant, I had strived to get close to the position I held in Oman and India. This was it. This was that moment when I got to where I deserved to be. If you are an immigrant and thinking of how improbable it is to win an award, you are right. It is a lot about luck. It is about being in the right place at the right time. You don't have to aspire for awards, though. You need to aspire to achieve back that reputation, status, and financial position that you governed before you moved here. You need to get to the reputation, status, and financial position that you thought you will get to when you moved to Canada. It is extremely easy to drop your arms and be caught-up in putting food on the table. It is even simpler to lose your self-confidence, but that's not what you should aim for. That's not what you came here for. You should keep challenging the norms. You need to keep asking why the entire gamut of skills you possess can't get you to the position you desire and deserve. The answer to those questions will take you out of the maze.

Coming back to my story! Amidst the celebrations that followed the award, I had forgotten about another story that was brewing at that time. One of my friend had nominated my name for the RBC's "TOP 25 Canadian Immigrants" Award for year 2013. At that point, I didn't really take it very seriously. Being nominated for the award was no joke. Some of the most renowned names in Canadian history have been nominated and won this award. Great people like Michaelle Jean, Deepa Mehta, Vasdev Chanchlani, Ian Hanomansingh, Jean Augustine, Olivia Chow, Jagjit Singh Hans (Tiger Jeet Singh), Arlene Dickinson, and others have received the honour of winning the title.

"Why would someone nominate me?" is what I thought. Hence, life moved on and I completely forgot about that. I didn't even care to find out the status of the nomination process. Why would I bother when I was certain that I was not going to be nominated? In the meantime, I won my 'Newcomer Gem Volunteer Award' and that consumed a large part of mind-space. However, one fine day; I received an email from the organization that shortlists and nominates candidates. I remember that I was at work when the email came in. I make it a point to not use my phone during my work hours, and hence I missed reading that email then. It was not until after I got home that the email drew my attention. The name of the sender caught my eye and so did the subject-line. That moment is frozen in time, and a permanent part of my family's memories. I was just entering my house with my phone in my hand. My wife got annoyed because I was engrossed in the phone when I should be greeting my family. However, all I could do was to pass on the phone to her and insist her to read. She jumped in joy and excitement. I was one of the top 75 people who were nominated for the award. This meant that I was going into the next phase of the selection process. I didn't bother reading about the selection process just yet. Instead, I wanted to digest this information first. I wanted to be sure about what I was reading.

"Can this be sent to me by mistake?" I asked my wife.

It definitely wasn't. The email had my name on it, and it was certainly meant for me. What a fabulous feeling! It was a feeling of unadulterated bliss.

When the excitement subsided, I found it worthwhile to go back and read through the entire email. So, I was one of the top 75 immigrants. The next step in the process was the one that could halt my journey towards the 'Top 25 Immigrants' status. The organization didn't want to take the onus of judging the value of any individual person's contribution to their community. They wanted to rather get people to have a say in the process. Those people, who believed in a candidate's ability, could vote for them. Why I thought it could halt my journey was because I was new to the country. In my brief stay in Canada, I had met with multiple people. However, I had very few real contacts to go back to. When I spoke at an event, for example, my audience will take down my contact information. However, I wouldn't have their contact. Although many people were inspired by my talks and volunteering work, but I didn't have the means of getting their contact and informing them about my candidature in this prestigious award. This meant that I had limited people I could go to; or at least that is what I thought.

So, I decided to start small. I sent out an email to those people that I knew. These were colleagues in Canada, my family in India, and other people whom I had tried to help in Oman. The objective was to engage these people and see what their response was. I wanted to explore if they were willing to help me and vote for me. To my surprise, the response was incredibly amazing. Most people in the list responded to me positively. In fact, quite a few of them cast their vote right away. That was a starting point. Many of these people offered to refer my name to other people. I was awed by this gesture and it was a validation of how much these people loved me. As the references came along, my network started to grow. I was making it a point to take a note of every person who was voting for me. Regardless of the result, I was obligated to them and I was going to send them a thank you note at the end of the process.

Another ray of hope came from India. I always knew that my father is a well-connected person, but I was never aware of the massive size of his network. There were people, all over the world, who now knew about my candidature and wanted me to receive credit for my work. They wanted to do their bit in helping me achieve an incredible milestone in my life.

Last but not the least, my community here in Canada started pitching in. As the word spread about my nomination among newcomers that I had helped, they started voting in huge numbers. Not only was this helping me get a step closer towards the award, it was also introducing me to a whole new list of people. I was being introduced to the potential of my work. They say; when you do a good deed, it comes back to you. I had tried to make a contribution, and it was all coming back to me.

With all this support and enthusiasm, was the award going to ever evade me? That day was here and the stage was ready. The list of the Top 25 Immigrants was being announced, and there it was. They announced my name. 'Sukhjit Singh' was now one of the Top 25 Immigrants. My name had never sounded as pleasant to me before. My excitement and happiness saw no bound. Being just 4 years old in the country, I was now a part of the prestigious group of immigrants who had made a difference. A couple of years ago, I was struggling to find a proper job for myself. Today, I was being felicitated for my work. Isn't this a validation of how much things can change in 4 years? Miracles do happen! From cold-calling in harsh Canadian winters to the cozy feeling of this award in my hands, a miracle had just happened.

That's why I think that we should never stop working hard. There are times when results refuse to come your way, but a day would arrive when you will get all that's due to you. You will certainly face hurdles and you might even fall on your face. You know what, though? Every time you fall, you get back up with more intensity. You continue to sweat it out, and you never know. Any one drop of your sweat can embellish the gloomy sky with a beautiful rainbow. So, keep dreaming and enjoy the journey!

CLOSING THOUGHTS
HAPPILY EVER AFTER

here are moments in life that leave you in a state of
trance. You are so happy and you celebrate so hard
that you can't feel anything else. That's a time when you are
at peace with yourself. That was how I felt when I won that
award that day. I was not thinking about how significant this
achievement was. I was not really thinking of what would
this bring to me. For now, I was Sukhjit Singh; one of the top
25 immigrants for that year. When I was driving back from
the award ceremony, my brain was silent and restful. I love
ideas, and my brain is generally populated with thousands of
thoughts at a time. However, that day I was just smiling. I
had achieved a level of recognition and respect that I had never
expected to get.

We got back home, and my wife put on my favourite Punjabi
music. The thing about Punjabi music is that it is always soulful.
It might be a peppy, dance number or a slow, romantic song;
but, it will always touch your soul. It emancipates you from all
the worries and all the other thoughts that keep us in captivity
in our day to day lives. Given the occasion, my wife chose

some popular dance numbers, and we danced. We danced like there was no tomorrow. I am generally very restrained, but I wasn't imprisoned that day by the fear of people judging me. That was partly due to the music, but also because it was one of the best days of my life till date. Bhangra (Punjabi folk dance) turned into Bollywood dancing turned into random anything. We danced for 2 hours straight before our feet refused to cooperate and we crashed into our bed. What a night it was! It was all falling in place. First the award, then the dancing, and finally 10 hours of deep sleep. What a night!

When I woke up was when some sanity finally set in. I still had a hangover of the previous night, and the high was here to stay. However, I was thinking a little more sensibly now. I started thinking of what that award meant to me and my life goal. My brain was again populated with thoughts and ideas about how I could use this distinction to improve my work and help more people in the community and beyond.

At this moment, I wish I could end this by saying 'I lived happily ever after.' I strongly believe that happiness is not momentary. It is, instead, a state of mind. You can't be sad at 9 a.m. when you start work, and be happy at 5 p.m. when you are done. If you are happy, you are happy! Yes; God has been kind and my life has progressed smoothly. However, I wouldn't make the mistake of believing that the award was an end. An 'end' represents when you breathe your list. Up until then, every achievement is a milestone. It is a milestone that leads you towards your ultimate destination, your life goal. Hence, that award was not the end but a new beginning. Since that award, I have continued to ideate and strive hard. I have continued to face road-blocks and my family has continued to be my pillar of support while tackling all those road-blocks and impediments.

We should all clearly identify milestones in our lives, and work towards those. Milestones help us plan better, and every time you get to one such milestone- take a break and enjoy it to the fullest. Memories of such enjoyment and celebrations help you strive harder for the future.

I have set out my milestones for the future and will hopefully have the pleasure to share more information about them with you soon. Till then, continue to be persistent as persistence certainly pays. It did with me!

Skilled Immigrant in Canada is:

Intelligent

Motivational

Meaningful

Innovative

Goal-oriented

Risk taker

Approachable

Necessary

Talented

CANADA 150

www. **SukhForChange**.com

VOLUNTEER

Vital

Opportunity

Learning

Understanding

Networking

Targeting

Empowering

Entertaining

Rewarding

www.SukhForChange.com

CANADA 150